VOICES OF THE NEW SPRINGTIME

VOICES OF THE NEW SPRINGTIME

The Life and Work of the Catholic Church in the 21st Century

Proceedings from the 25th Annual Conference of the
Fellowship of Catholic Scholars

September 27–29, 2002
Philadelphia, Pennsylvania

Edited by Kenneth D. Whitehead

ST. AUGUSTINE'S PRESS
South Bend, Indiana
2004

Manufactured in the United States of America.

1 2 3 4 5 6   10 09 08 07 06 05 04

Library of Congress Cataloging in Publication Data
Fellowship of Catholic Scholars. Convention (25th: 2002:
    Philadelphia, Pa.)
    Voices of the new springtime : the life and work of the
    Catholic Church in the 21st century / edited by Kenneth D.
    Whitehead. – 1st ed.
        p. cm.
    "Proceedings from the 25th Annual Conference of the
    Fellowship of Catholic Scholars, September 27–29, 2002,
    Philadelphia, Pennsylvania."
    ISBN 1-58731-900-4 (pbk.: alk. paper)
    1. Catholic Church – United States – Congresses.
    I. Whitehead, K. D. II. Title.
BX1404.F45 2004
282'.73'0905 – dc22   2004011470

*∞ The paper used in this publication meets the minimum requirements of
the American National Standard for Information Sciences – Permanence of
Paper for Printed Materials, ANSI Z39.48 – 1984.*

CONTENTS

INTRODUCTION

The theme for the 25th anniversary convention of the Fellowship of Catholic Scholars, "Voices of the New Springtime: The Life and Work of the Catholic Church in the 21st Century," was chosen before the serial public revelations of the sex abuse in the Church began in January, 2002, and continued through the year, turning our 25th anniversary year into a year of acute crisis and anxiety for the Church – what some have termed "the long lent of 2002." The whole thing inevitably put something of a damper on our thoughts and hopes for a new "Springtime" for the faith; and, understandably, the crisis has been one of great sorrow and concern for the Fellowship and its members. That any children at any time could be harmed within the confines of the Church of Christ is an acutely painful thing; that even a tiny minority of those ordained to preach and act in persona Christi could have engaged in the kind of sinful and evil conduct which endangered or harmed children and others – not to speak of the harm to themselves and their own souls – was even worse.

Similarly disappointing, surely, to all Fellowship members – who specifically affirm by the fact of their membership their obedience to legitimate Church authority and their adherence to the authentic teachings of the Church's magisterium – was the overwhelming public evidence that, in this crisis, we were unable to depend upon those whom "the Holy Spirit has made guardians . . . to feed the Church of the Lord" (Acts 20:28), namely, our bishops. We have no desire to do anything but uphold the legitimate authority of the bishops; but it is evident that by the actions of many of them – or perhaps even more by their inactions in some crucial respects! – the bishops have unfortunately allowed grave harm to be done to the Church and to the faith, harm which may not either soon or easily be remedied.

Certainly the bishops' Charter for the Protection of Children and Young People, approved in final form at their annual meeting in November, 2002, is a worthy start on treating the maladies that have now been publicly shown to infect the Church. In the light of all that has been revealed about the actions of some of the Church's members and leaders in the course of the year 2002, however, it surely cannot be considered more than a start. Much work – and prayer, and penance – remain.

Although the continuing crisis of 2002 was necessarily and inevitably much on the minds of those members of the Fellowship who assembled in Philadelphia for our 25th anniversary convention, the gathering itself nevertheless proceeded according to our chosen theme, and featured the prepared talks of our invited speakers elaborating in various ways on this theme. No formal attention was thus given to the crisis of 2002 at the convention beyond an interesting panel discussion concerning the prospects for a *plenary council* suggested by a number of bishops. Such a plenary council would be a truly collegial gathering of the bishops, and would empower them to legislate particular law for the Church in the United States (with the approval of the Holy See) in a way that the work of their regular Conference cannot match. Some claim it would also free the bishops from undue dependence on their staffs. The intended purpose of such a plenary council would be to address the root causes of the crisis and meet the challenge which Pope John Paul II placed on the American hierarchy when he called on them in April to use the crisis of 2002 as a means of the purification of the entire Catholic community – with, as an end result, "a holier priesthood, a holier episcopate, and a holier Church." This is an outcome we must truly hope for and pray for.

As for our chosen convention theme, though, it certainly proved to be a solid antidote to the bad news that had too often seemed to fill the year. By September we were badly in need of some Voices of the New Springtime. A new "springtime" of the faith has, of course, been a recurring theme of Pope John Paul II's. And the theme was, of course, adopted partly for that reason. In his *Tertio Millennio Adveniente* announcing the Jubilee Year, for example, the Holy Father spoke both of a new "springtime of Christian life" (#18) in the 21st century and of a "true springtime of the spirit" (#46). Similarly, in his *ad limina* address to the U.S. bishops on October 24, 1998, the pope spoke of the "springtime of hope" which Christianity offers as a counterpoint to the century of tears just passed. Again, in his Angelus message for March 25, 2001, John Paul II called for a "new springtime of life with respect and acceptance of every human being in whose face shines the image of Christ." These are only a few of the pope's references to the theme of a "springtime" that can and must give us new hope.

It was in this positive vein that our speakers addressed the topics – especially pertinent today – of faith and reason, Catholic higher education, lay action, Christian feminism, the media, and secularism and democracy. We are proud to present the texts of these talks by these excellent speakers in the present volume. We are particularly proud that His Eminence Avery Cardinal Dulles was willing to keynote the convention, and also that our principal awardee this year, the outstanding pro-life Pennsylvania law-maker, Senator Rick Santorum, was present on his own home grounds in Philadelphia to receive the award and grace the occasion with his own moving words.

KEYNOTE ADDRESS
THE VOICE OF REASON AND OF FAITH
Avery Cardinal Dulles, s.j.

Let me begin by congratulating the Fellowship of Catholic Scholars on attaining the mature age of twenty-five. By coincidence, as we heard this afternoon, today is also the feast day of St. Vincent de Paul, making it the patronal feast of the Congregation of the Mission, to which Father David O'Connell belongs. As a Jesuit, I might remark that on this very day the Society of Jesus celebrates the 462nd anniversary of its first approval by the Holy See. Since Vatican II our Society has gone through most of the difficulties experienced by the priesthood in the United States. But with the help of stalwarts like Earl Weiss and Ken Baker, former presidents of your Fellowship, we Jesuits may be able to weather the storm. I am convinced that we are approaching a new springtime, thanks to an army of younger Jesuits typified by Father Peter Ryan, who just introduced me.

I well remember that in 1975 and 1976 there were murmurings from a few of the more conservative members of the Catholic Theological Society of America that they were planning to leave and found a separate organization. As President of the CTSA at that time, I felt it my duty to urge them to remain in the Theological Society on the ground that their withdrawal would be a loss, leaving the more liberal and radical elements in unfettered control. But I could well understand why the more loyal and traditional Catholics felt frustrated. They were rarely elected to office and were rarely asked to give major addresses. When policy decisions were made at the annual business meetings, conservatives were regularly outvoted. In 1977, the year when this Fellowship was founded, the CTSA was instrumental in the publication of the notorious book, *Human Sexuality*, which had been commissioned by its Board of Directors some five years earlier.

The Fellowship performed an important service in this nation by assembling a body of serious Catholic scholars who supported the Catholic tradition and the magisterium of the Church rather than habitually contesting them. While that service cannot be the sole purpose of your organization, the Church will continue to depend on your organization to perform it for the foreseeable future.

The Fellowship differs from the CTSA, not only in its fidelity to ecclesiastical authority, but also in its scope. In addition to theologians, it includes members who are, for example, philosophers, historians, sociologists, and canon and civil lawyers. This interdisciplinary character is, I believe, an advantage because these other disciplines need one another, and need theology for their own health, just as theology, conversely, needs to be in conversation with them.

The Fellowship has sometimes been accused of factionalism and divisiveness. I do not know whether there may have been something to the accusation in past years, but in any case the roster of speakers and choice of themes for this convention gives no grounds for it. The program indicates to me that your fundamental aims are inclusively Catholic and constructive. The program for this meeting declares that you are committing yourselves anew to being one of those associations that Pope John Paul II describes as continuing "to give the Church a vitality that is God's gift and a true 'springtime of the Spirit.'"[1]

In a letter of March 23, 2002, your president, Father Thomas F. Dailey, OSFS, invited me to address you on the question "how the Church can appeal to all people as the voice of reason and of faith." In my presentation I shall reverse the order of the two terms, proceeding from faith to reason, as we theologians are prone to do.

The Call to Evangelize

That the Church is the voice of faith is obvious to everyone. The Church has received from Christ the mission to preach the good news of redemption to every creature under heaven. Paul VI made it clear, in his reflections on Vatican II, that the first task of the Church is to evangelize, to spread the gospel. John Paul II has exemplified this priority in his personal conduct and has persistently exhorted the Church to engage in an evangelization that is new in its ardor, its methods, and its expression.[2] "Missionary evangelization," he declares, "is the primary service which the Church can render to every individual and to all humanity in the modern world."[3] From this I infer that to exclude any human group from the Church's proclamation would be a betrayal of the Church's mandate. Although evangelization takes different forms when directed to Jews and to Gentiles, neither of these groups should be cut off from Christian proclamation.

By and large, Catholics, at least in this country, have been sluggish in responding to the Pope's appeal. Evangelization teams complain that they get little support from parishes and dioceses. The behavior of Catholics seems to belie the Church's claim to have a message intended for everyone who comes into the world. Fundamentalist and Pentecostal churches put us to shame by their missionary zeal, even though we may not fully approve of their missionary tactics or their understanding of the gospel.

Many reasons can help to account for the apparent apathy of the Catholic community. The energies of bishops and priests have been taken up with internal problems of administration and pastoral care, leaving them little time and few resources for spreading the faith. The Catholic community suffers from internal tensions, sometimes amounting to a kind of spiritual schism. And in American society there are many pressures, social, economic, and legal, against evangelization. But perhaps the most fundamental difficulty comes from erroneous understandings of faith and reason, and of the relations between them.

The Concept of Faith

Since the days of Immanuel Kant, the Western world has been dominated by the assumption that there can be no real knowledge, or intellectual assurance, about anything that transcends the world of ordinary experience. When faith is not dismissed as a childish superstition, it is regarded as an irrational sentiment of the heart or an unfounded decision of the will rather than as genuine cognition. Religion is consigned to the private arena and excluded from the public square. Like music and poetry, it is seen as a leisure occupation for those who have a taste for it. Public institutions are supposed to operate on purely secular principles, taking no cognizance of any religious point of view.

Consistently with this outlook, faith would have no legitimate place in the university, which is concerned with knowledge, not sentiment. In most non-Catholic universities, theology, if it survives at all, has been exiled to the divinity school, where it is treated as a practical discipline for the training of ministers. Some secular universities admit religious studies, which deal with religion as a social phenomenon, but they examine it only by the methods of disciplines such as history, sociology, and psychology. They abstain from normative considerations based on Christian revelation.

Theologians themselves, not excluding some who are reputed to be Catholic, have all too often gone along with the description of faith as non-cognitive, or at least as having no objectifiable content. Within this school, George Lindbeck has delineated two models.[4] The first, which he calls "experiential-expressive," describes faith as an existential response to a mysterious encounter with absolute transcendence – an experience devoid of all definable content. On the ground that the experience is apophatic, this model denies that faith has any doctrinal content. If Christians hold and teach certain doctrines, these teachings are separable from faith and ought not to be confused with it. They are best understood as symbols or metaphors pointing in the direction of the ineffable. This non-doctrinal conception of faith gives a license to believers to dispute every dogma of the Church on the ground that it cannot possibly be a matter of faith.

The second model, which Lindbeck describes as "cultural-linguistic," criticizes the first as being too subjectivist and individualist. It seeks to respect the social and traditional character of religion. Holding that the acceptance of doctrines is essential to any given faith, this second model depicts doctrines as rules of speech that must be observed in the faith-community. Scriptures and doctrines tell the story on which the community is grounded. Doctrines are held to be "intra-systematically" true but not necessarily ontologically true. To illustrate what he means by this distinction, Lindbeck states that the statement "Hamlet lived in Denmark" is true within the framework of Shakespeare's play, but need not be true in actual fact. So, likewise, the proposition "Jesus is Lord," is true for Christians, in the sense that it coheres with the Christian story.

This second model, while agreeing with the first that faith is non-cognitive, differs from it in giving faith a voice and a language. But like the first, it denies that Church doctrine can claim, as such, to represent objective realities. Doctrine becomes a code for speech within a community that is content to be sectarian. Members of the faith community, sharing a common language, can communicate with one another but cannot give reasons why nonmembers ought to join their community.

The two models I have described are alike in denying that faith pertains to the realm of knowledge, a domain that they relinquish to secular reason. Faith, on these theories, cannot possibly come into conflict with reason because it makes no claims to objective truth. While faith thus makes itself immune to rational criticism, its security is purchased at a heavy price. Lacking any objective reference, faith can make no impact on human society or on scientific learning. People pursuing worldly occupations feel entitled to dismiss faith as irrelevant.

Subjectivism and relativism are alien to traditionally Catholic conceptions of faith. The truth of faith requires that it correspond with reality and have validity for all times and places. In a sense every truth is universal and permanent. Once the Twin Towers of the World Trade Center have collapsed, it remains eternally true that they were destroyed on a certain notorious date. The past cannot be undone. However unpredictable the event was, those who thought it would not happen were wrong. The event proved that their expectations were untrue.

Similarly, it is true for all people at all times that the Second Person of the Blessed Trinity would, or did, become man in Jesus Christ, that he would die, or did die, on the cross and rise from the dead. There is nothing subjective about these affirmations. If we believe them at all, we must hold them to be true for everyone.

Subjectivism in religion makes no more sense than subjectivism in geography. The existence of the continents we call North and South America did not depend on their discovery by European explorers or by anyone else. So, too, the divine essence subsists in three persons, whether anyone believes it or not.

In reacting against this agnosticism, some Christians – Evangelical Protestants and. less frequently, Catholics – fall into an exaggerated rationalism. Neglecting the need for the light of grace and the favorable inclination of the will, they speak as though faith were an achievement of reason alone. In defending objectivity, they tend to depict God as an object that can be contained within human categories, ignoring the cautions of Holy Scripture about the inapproachable light in which God dwells (1 Tim 6:16). In the words of

Vatican I, "Divine mysteries by their nature so excel the created intellect that, even when they have been communicated in revelation and received in faith, they remain covered by the veil of faith itself and shrouded as it were in darkness as long as in this mortal life 'we are away from the Lord . . .'" (DS 3016).

Revelation gives us only a very fragmentary glimpse of the God whom we serve, but revealed truth is not, for all that, uncertain. Although we cannot be fully convinced of, and fully committed to, the truth of the gospel without the light of grace, that light does not make the message of the gospel true. It simply permits us to recognize its truth and live accordingly.

In recent decades there has been a great deal of confusion about propositional truths. The truths of Christian faith, some contend, are not propositional. We may concede that faith is much more than an assent to a set of propositions, but we cannot deny that some propositions are to be held as matters of faith. As Christians we confess our faith by reciting the creed. The declarative sentences of the creed and of Christian dogma represent affirmations to which Christians must agree under pain of ceasing to be members of the community of faith.

Those of us who wish to be orthodox in our faith must confront this philosophical challenge head-on, so that Catholics may evangelize with the voice of faith. We must insist that there are truths of faith, revealed truths, capable of being formulated in propositions. Subjectivists and relativists are neither good Christians nor effective apostles. They are unable to show why faith should appeal to all people.

The Voice of Reason

It is more difficult to see why the Church should speak with the voice of reason. Our civilization almost instinctively adopts the view of Kant that faith begins where reason leaves off. Reality therefore becomes divided into two spheres: a world of measurable realities that can be encompassed by reason and, vaguely hovering above it, a world of faith about which reason can say nothing. The first of these worlds is public, the second private. In this schematization, secular society is considered to be autonomous. Economics, sociology, and politics claim to have their own laws, which have no more to do with religion than mathematics has. The various disciplines in the academy and the various professions in society want to pursue their own agenda without interference from religion. Precisely because religion, as we Catholics understand it, makes truth-claims, secular academicians resent it and resist its influence.

The Lutheran theologian Dietrich Bonhoeffer took up arms against the prevalent dualism. In his *Ethics*, a book left incomplete when he was arrested by the Gestapo in 1943, he forthrightly proclaimed: "He [Jesus Christ] is the center and strength of the Bible, of the Church, and of theology, but also of humanity, of reason, of justice, and of culture. Everything must return to Him; it is only under His protection that it can live."[5]

The Church loves and cherishes reason as a crowning gift of God's creative love. Reason, as the property that most fundamentally distinguishes human beings from all other creatures, lies at the root of human freedom and dignity. The Church seeks to sustain reason and raise it up through the leaven of faith. Reason prepares the way to faith, and when faith is attained, reason helps the believer to understand what is believed. Faith and reason, in combination, enable the human spirit to soar to heavenly heights, preparing it for eternal blessedness. Divorced from faith, reason falters and becomes enmeshed in error.

It is not enough to address the relationship between faith and reason in the abstract. Far more pressing is the concrete problem of rightly relating the gospel and culture. This is the problem raised by Bonhoeffer in the passage just cited and even more persistently by John Paul II. At the very outset of his pontificate, he challenged the nations of the world: "Do not be afraid. Open wide the doors for Christ. To his saving power open the boundaries of states, economic and political systems, the vast fields of culture, civilization, and development."[6] The pope's first encyclical began with the sentence: "the Redeemer of man, Jesus Christ, is the centre of the universe and of history."[7] He radiates the conviction that the gospel speaks to a deep and ineradicable need for individual and social redemption. The great worlds of economics and politics, as well as the inner worlds of sin and conscience, require the light and love of Christ.

Human society, according to the pope, cannot find peace and justice without unselfish love and forgiveness. But altruistic love and forgiveness are hardly possible without a religious motivation. Hannah Arendt, a secular Jewish intellectual, acknowledged that

Jesus of Nazareth was the first to call attention to the role of forgiveness in the realm of human affairs.[8] His insight, she observed,
needs to be built into group relationships. Without forgiveness the
evils of the past continue to weigh heavily on the present. Going
beyond what Arendt says, I submit that the world will never find
peace and justice unless it embraces, at least implicitly, the principles
brought into the world by Christ, the Prince of Peace.

Faith and the University

Many of you are involved in Catholic universities. If faith is non-
cognitive, as some hold it to be, a Catholic university would be a
contradiction in terms, and some maintain that in fact it is. Since a
university, as John Henry Newman insisted, is a place of universal
knowledge, faith could have no place in it unless it were cognitive.
But because faith does have a content that is objectively true and
revealed, universities can and should be open to it.

Pope John Paul II has shown that Catholic universities have a
great advantage in being able to draw on the wisdom of the eternal
Logos, revealed through the Incarnation and preserved and enriched
by centuries of reflection.[9] Far from limiting the freedom of the university, Catholic faith liberates the university from the dark valley
where the light of revelation does not shine. To operate without benefit of revelation is for a university a handicap. The centrality of
Christ, the supreme Truth, gives Catholic universities an invaluable
resource for overcoming the intellectual fragmentation that besets
most universities today.

The dominion of Christ as the Word of God leaves intact the
inherent laws and finality of human disciplines such as philosophy,
history, sociology, economics, law, and politics. It encourages these
disciplines to grow to their very limits, at which point they will find
that they need assistance from beyond themselves, and will be dis-
posed to accept the added light of revelation. In following their own
immanent logic, these disciplines paradoxically come up against the
need for their own conversion.

In his encyclical on Faith and Reason, John Paul II illustrates this
dialectical relationship with regard to philosophy and theology. He
depicts philosophy as a journey of discovery which cannot reach its
goal without embracing the revelation of truth that is in Jesus Christ.
"What human reason seeks `without knowing it' (cf. Acts 17:23) can

be found only through Jesus Christ: what is revealed in Him is 'the full truth' (cf. Jn 1:14–16) of everything which was created in him and through him and which therefore in him finds its fulfillment (cf. Col 1:17)."[10] He calls upon philosophers to return to their original vocation, which was to love and pursue wisdom. He urges them to recover a dynamic philosophy of being "which allows a full and comprehensive openness to reality as a whole, surpassing every limit in order to reach the One who brings all things to fulfillment."[11] Contact with revelation, he asserts, does not injure philosophy but on the contrary stirs it "to explore paths which of itself it would not even have suspected it could take."[12] In the search for truth philosophy and theology support one another. Philosophy illuminates the path toward truth; theology bears witness to the word of him who is Truth; and philosophy, once again, assists theology in understanding God's word.

Interdisciplinary Dialogue

An analogous relationship to revealed truth, I believe, can be found in other disciplines that concern themselves with the deepest reality of creation and human existence. Psychology must take account of the aspiration of the human spirit for union with God, which alone can fully heal it from its ills. Psychotherapy must at a certain point make contact with what some have called "Christotherapy" – the healing influence of Christ through word, sacrament, and prayer. Genetic research, as currently practiced, raises complex ethical and religious questions that cannot be responsibly answered without the input of faith.

History as an academic discipline cannot insulate itself from revelation, for it cannot permanently evade the realities of sacred history, in which God has acted in meaningful ways. The quest for the historical Jesus cannot be conducted on merely secular methodological principles, because those principles are by their own admission incapable of acknowledging the supernatural. To grasp the reality of the Incarnation and the Resurrection, or to perceive the truth of the apostolic witness, the historian has to go beyond the limits of mere secular historiography. Otherwise the historian will be tempted to dismiss facts that his discipline cannot handle.

John Henry Newman, in his *The Idea of a University,* takes this line of consideration much further than I can do on this occasion. He shows, for example, why disciplines such as economics and medicine go astray if they are divorced from theology. Where theology is absent, he points out, other disciplines are tempted to move into the vacuum and answer theological questions by their own methods, which are unsuited to the task. Today Newman might point out that astrophysicists who lack adequate training in metaphysics and theology should not try to pronounce on the existence of God and the fact of creation.

If the various disciplines are to coexist in a fruitful relationship, each must enjoy a certain autonomy, follow its own proper method, and acknowledge its own limitations. For mutual assistance to take place, each must be willing to learn from the others as well as to instruct them. The economist profits from psychology, the lawyer from history, the literary critic from sociology, and so forth. Theology, we must believe, has its proper place within this republic of disciplines. It makes use of a great variety of disciplines such as literary criticism, critical history, and psychology. In drawing on these resources, theologians must take great care not to be misled by the nonreligious and antireligious biases of some experts in these fields. That is an important reason for bringing orthodox believers into Catholic universities where they can engage in dialogue with other scholars who share their faith.

One of the things that has drawn many people like myself to the Church is the culture-forming capacity of Catholic Christianity. I observed this especially in my studies in medieval history, when the barbarism of the invaders was tamed and the Greek and Latin classics were preserved in the monasteries and cathedral schools. Thanks to the benign influence of the Church, a high civilization came into being. Painting and sculpture, architecture and music, lyric and epic poetry, philosophy and law entered into a harmonious chorus under the direction of Catholic faith. The Reformation, while it did not sweep everything away, failed to produce any comparable culture. It led rather to secularization and fragmentation. Western civilization, having rejected Christ as its guiding norm, continues to drift without any overarching vision capable of setting in order the immense forces of human creativity.

My hope would be for Catholic agencies, especially colleges and universities, to demonstrate once again that religious faith can give inspiration and direction to the arts and sciences. Although we have much to learn from secular institutions, we should not simply envy or mimic them. We need to strike out on our own and produce samples of Catholic philosophy, jurisprudence, poetry, theater, literature, music, and visual art. Because of the inroads of secularism, these religiously inspired cultural achievements are almost totally lacking in today's world, but there is no reason why they cannot be revived.

As an inclusive Fellowship of Catholic Scholars, your society can help to foster this many-faceted renewal of Catholic culture, enabling the Church, as the voice of faith and reason, gospel and culture, to make a broader and more effective appeal to the men and women of our time. The challenge is immense, but the possibilities are fascinating and, to some of us, all but irresistible.

Avery Cardinal Dulles, S.J., is currently the Laurence J. McGinley Professor of Religion and Society at Fordham University, a position that he has held since 1988. An internationally known author and lecturer, he graduated from Harvard College in 1940, and spent a year and a half in the Harvard Law School before serving in the United States Navy, emerging with the rank of lieutenant.

Avery Dulles entered the Jesuit Order, and was ordained to the priesthood in 1956. After a year in Germany, he studied at the Gregorian University in Rome, and was awarded the Doctorate in Sacred Theology in 1960. He was created a Cardinal of the Roman Church on February 21, 2001, by Pope John Paul II.

The author of over 650 articles on theological topics, Cardinal Dulles has published twenty-one books, including *Models of the Church* (1974), *Models of Revelation* (1983), *The Catholicity of the Church* (1985), *The Craft of Theology: From Symbol to System* (1992), *The Assurance of Things Hoped For: A Theology of Christian Faith* (1994), *The Splendor of Faith: The Theological Vision of Pope John Paul II* (1999), and his latest book, *The New World of Faith* (2000).

Past President of both the Catholic Theological Society of America and the American Theological Society, he is presently a consultor to the Committee on Doctrine of the U.S. Conference of Catholic Bishops and an Associate Fellow of the Woodstock Theological Center in Washington, D.C. He has an impressive collection of awards, including Phi Beta Kappa, the Croix de Guerre, the Cardinal Spellman Award for Distinguished Achievement in

Theology, the Boston College Presidential Bicentennial Award, the Religious Education Forum Award from the National Catholic Education Association, *America* magazine's Campion Award, the F. Sadlier Dinger Award for Contributions to the Catechetical Ministry of the Church, and twenty-one honorary doctorates.

Notes

1   John Paul II, Apostolic Letter *Novo millennio ineunte*, §46.

2   John Paul II, at Port-au-Prince, Haiti, March 9, 1983, "The Task of the Latin American Bishop," *Origins* 12 (March 24, 1983): 659–62, at 661. John Paul's program for "the new evangelization" is heavily indebted to Paul VI's Apostolic Exhortation *Evangelii nuntiandi* (1975).

3   John Paul II, Encyclical *Redemptoris missio*, 2.

4   George Lindbeck, *The Nature of Doctrine* (Philadelphia: Westminster, 1983).

5   Dietrich Bonhoeffer, *Ethics* (New York: Macmillan Paperback edition, 1965), 56.

6   John Paul II, Inauguration Homily, October 22, 1978; *Origins* 8 (November 2, 1978): 305–8, at 307–8.

7   John Paul II, *Redemptor hominis*, 1.

8   Hannah Arendt, *The Human Condition: A Study of the Central Conditions Facing Modern Man* (Garden City, N.Y.: Doubleday, 1959), 238.

9   See John Paul II, Apostolic Constitution *Ex Corde Ecclesiae*, 16.

10 John Paul II, *Fides et ratio*, 34.

11 *Ibid.*, 97.

12 *Ibid.*, 73.

A NEW SPRINGTIME IN CATHOLIC HIGHER EDUCATION
Very Rev. David M. O'Connell, C.M., J.C.D.

Today is the feast of St. Vincent de Paul (1580–1660), the founder of the Congregation to which I belong. Although St. Vincent is not recognized for any particular contribution to higher learning apart from the reform of seminaries in 17th century France, his apostolic zeal continues to inspire the members of the Church who seek to be faithful to the Gospel of Christ in the work they do. His community, the Congregation of the Mission, or "Vincentians," sponsors three Catholic institutions of higher learning, two of which – St. John's University in New York and DePaul University in Chicago – are the largest Catholic universities in the United States. I ask for his intercession today on behalf of all of us who gather to celebrate the work of Catholic higher education advanced through the efforts of this Fellowship.

For twenty-five years, the Fellowship of Catholic Scholars has promoted the Catholic intellectual tradition, the "Catholic difference" referred to by Father Thomas Dailey in the spring edition of the Fellowship *Quarterly*.[1] During the past five of those twenty-five years, I have had the privilege of serving as president of The Catholic University of America in Washington, D.C., the national university of the Catholic Church in our country. It is from the perspective of a Catholic university president and president of that particular institution that I wish to address you this afternoon.

The theme for our gathering is "Voices for A New Springtime," drawing upon the emphasis provided by our Holy Father Pope John Paul II in several of his more recent writings, in particular his apostolic letters for the Jubilee Year 2000, *Tertio Millenio Adveniente*[2] and *Novo Millennio Ineunte*.[3] It is an appropriate theme as we move forward into the 21st century. I do believe that Catholic higher education is, indeed, experiencing a "new springtime." The latter half of the 20th century, however, might be more accurately labeled not a "new springtime" but – to borrow the title of a work by American novelist John Steinbeck taken from Shakespeare's *Richard III* – "the winter of our discontent" in Catholic higher education.

In 1955, Monsignor John Tracy Ellis, professor of Church history at The Catholic University of America, wrote a scathing criticism of the quality of American Catholic intellectual life in a paper that he delivered at the annual meeting of the Catholic Commission on Intellectual and Cultural Affairs in St. Louis. In his presentation, later published in the Fordham University journal *Thought*, Ellis gave voice to the belief noted in a popular text of his day on American institutions that:

> . . . in no western society is the intellectual prestige of Catholicism lower than in the country where, in such respects as wealth, numbers and strength of organization, it is so powerful.[4]

Ellis went on to observe that:

> No well-informed American Catholic in this country will attempt to challenge that statement. Admittedly, the weakest aspect of the Church in this country lies in its failure to produce national leaders and to exercise commanding influence in intellectual circles, and this at a time when the numbers of Catholics in the United States . . . and their material resources are incomparably superior to those of any other branch of the universal Church.[5]

Ellis presented these ideas almost fifty years ago. If his stinging indictment were considered to be true *at* that time or *up to* that time, we should wonder why. Much of the fault, I believe, lay not so much in a fear that Catholic scholars demonstrated for Church authorities, as some have argued; but it lay, rather, in a fear of the judgments of their secular academic counterparts. The lack of courage to present the teachings of the Church with conviction in their inherent truth within a broader scholarly community evidenced a not too subtle belief among our own Catholic scholars that religious faith, and scholarly activity based upon it, was an embarrassment that relegated Catholic intellectuals to a second class status. Faith, after all, was considered in the secular arena to be the true enemy of reason in an "enlightened" intellectual world.

There was, no one can honestly doubt, an anti-Catholic prejudice at work in the United States from the time of its foundation and a genuine hostility "to all things Catholic," as Monsignor Ellis noted.[6] Even Harvard professor Arthur M. Schlesinger, Sr., once labeled "bias against your Church as the most persistent prejudice in the history of the American people."[7] For that reason, among others, much of the energy within the American Catholic community in general, and the American Catholic professorate in particular, during the late 19th and early 20th centuries was devoted to "apologetics" rather than to pure scholarly endeavor. The audience to which they made their appeals was largely an immigrant population that did not place primary value on Catholic intellectual advancement, let alone creating great Catholic institutions of higher learning. One needs look no further than the history of The Catholic University of America to verify that assertion.[8] The concept of a national Catholic research university was hotly debated within the American hierarchy itself. And yet, although visible efforts were made by many within the Catholic academy to promote Catholic higher education as their existing colleges expanded into universities, as late as 1938 the challenge was presented to the Church and Catholic scholars that "research cannot be the primary object of a Catholic graduate school because it is at war with the whole Catholic life of the mind."[9] American Catholic "universities" were popularly viewed as concerned not so much with the penetration of truth as they were with passing on a given tradition of truth, the Catholic tradition, in which little in the way of addition, alteration or development was deemed necessary.[10] It was an unfortunate perception that higher education within the American Catholic academic community was an "either/or" proposition rather than a "both/and." one.

When Ellis authored his now famous essay, he had no idea that a Vatican Council would soon be convened to address the situation of the Church in the modern world. The pope who would call for that Council was still the cardinal archbishop of Venice. When he assumed the papacy in the fall of 1958, and a year later announced the 21st ecumenical council, Pope John XXIII would usher in a new era in the history of the Catholic Church and with it, a new urgency to reform its structures and institutions throughout the world. Catholic higher education was not spared the effects of this "*aggiornamento.*"

In his apostolic constitution *Humanae salutis* convening the Council, Pope John XXIII wrote that the Church at that moment was:

> . . . witnessing a crisis under way within society. While humanity is on the edge of a new era, tasks of immense gravity and amplitude await the Church, as in its most tragic periods of history. It is a question in fact of bringing the modern world into contact with the vivifying and perennial energies of the gospel, a world which exalts itself with its conquests in the technical and scientific fields, but which brings also the consequences of a temporal order which some have wished to reorganize excluding God. This is why modern society is earmarked by a great material progress to which there is no corresponding advance in the moral field.[11]

The Holy Father addressed the hierarchy gathered in Council on October 11, 1962, stating that "the greatest concern of the Ecumenical Council is this: that the sacred deposit of Christian doctrine should be guarded and taught more efficaciously."[12] Guarded and *taught*!

That concern, as it related to Catholic institutions of higher learning, had been voiced some thirty-one years earlier by Pope Pius XI in his apostolic constitution *Deus Scientiarum Dominus,* where he wrote that the Church's chief concern in all of Catholic education had always been the correct *teaching* of doctrine.[13] Anyone well acquainted with Church teaching and its development in history could hardly argue that this process was ever, or could ever be, legitimately envisioned as a static enterprise.

The Fathers of the Second Vatican Council (1962–1965) dealt specifically with the broad topic of formal Catholic education in their 1965 declaration *Gravissimum educationis*. It has been said that the underlying concern of the Council was "education," "Catholic education" in one form or another.[14] The situation of Catholic universities and colleges received specific attention. The declaration stated that

> The Church is preoccupied too with schools of higher learning, especially colleges and universities and their faculties. In schools of this sort which are dependent upon her, she seeks in a systematic way to have individual branches of knowledge studied according to their own proper principles

and methods, and with due freedom of scientific investiga-
tion. She intends thereby to promote an ever deeper understanding of these fields, and as a result of extremely precise
evaluation of modern problems and inquiries, to have it
seen more profoundly how faith and reason give harmonious witness to the unity of all truth. The Church pursues
such a goal after the manner of her most illustrious teachers, especially St. Thomas Aquinas. The hoped-for result is
that the Christian mind may achieve, as it were, a public,
persistent and universal presence in the whole enterprise of
advancing higher culture, and that students of these institutions may become men (and women) truly outstanding in
learning, ready to shoulders society's heavier burdens and
to witness the faith to the world.[15]

One should notice the emphasis given here to proper disciplinary
methodology, due freedom of inquiry, growth in understanding, students outstanding in learning, advancing higher culture, and *witness
to faith.*

During the years immediately following the Second Vatican
Council, Catholic universities and colleges throughout the world
engaged in an effort to define their nature and mission in the Church
and world more clearly. That process witnessed the eager participation of members of the American Catholic academy, chastised as
they had been by Monsignor Ellis over ten years earlier.

In 1967, a gathering of Catholic educators in Land O' Lakes,
Wisconsin, sponsored by the International Federation of Catholic
Universities (IFCU), produced a document that set forth its own
credo on the nature of Catholic colleges and universities:

The Catholic university today must be a university in the
full modern sense of the word, with a strong commitment to
and concern for academic excellence. To perform its teaching and research function effectively, the Catholic university must have a true autonomy and academic freedom in the
face of authority of whatever kind, lay or clerical external
to the academic community itself. To say this is simply to
assert that institutional autonomy and academic freedom
are essential conditions of life and growth and indeed of
survival for Catholic universities as for all universities. The
Catholic university participates in the total life of our time,

has the same functions as all other true universities and, in general, offers the same services to society.[16]

Notice the emphasis given to authority "external to the academic community itself." This phrase was the "winter wind" as the stage was now set for what would become a decades-long effort to resolve growing contemporary tensions between the teaching Church and Catholic institutions of higher learning that existed in a variety of forms within its embrace in the post-conciliar era. Other international meetings would continue to occur but nowhere, at least in my opinion, were these tensions as keenly felt as within the American Catholic academic community.

The controversy surrounding the publication of Pope Paul VI's encyclical *Humanae Vitae*[17] in 1968, again in my opinion, distracted educators from the process of addressing the issue of the nature and purpose of Catholic institutions of higher education. In the minds of some, however, especially in the United States, *Humanae Vitae* was precisely the type of Church teaching that provided a timely example with which to frame the debate. Dissent over this encyclical crystallized the polarization between the faithful presentation and teaching of Church doctrine that Pope John XXIII saw as the "greatest concern" of the Council he convened, and "the true autonomy and academic freedom in the face of authority of whatever kind" that was the mantra of those who subscribed to the assertions of the Land O' Lakes manifesto. The "winter of our discontent" would continue. In many respects, The Catholic University of America at the time was the epicenter of the storm.

In 1972, at the invitation of the Holy See and IFCU, Catholic universities and colleges were invited to send delegates to an international congress in Rome, the second such gathering in Rome since Land O' Lakes. Their deliberations resulted in a document, "The Catholic University in the Modern World,"[18] which accomplished two major things: 1) it defined six basic types of Catholic post-secondary institutions that existed within the Church:

(a) Those directly established by ecclesiastical authorities and those which were not; and

(b) Those with statutory relationships to ecclesiastical authorities and those which had none; and

(c) Those with a formal, explicit commitment to Church teaching and beliefs and those whose commitment was merely implicit.

It also (2) provided a framework for Catholic identity and mission later cited by Pope John Paul II in his apostolic constitution *Ex Corde Ecclesiae.*[19]

Responding to this document, the Prefect of the Congregation for Catholic Education at that time, Cardinal Gabriel Marie Garrone, wrote that although the statement envisioned the existence of Catholic institutions of higher learning without formally established or statutory links to ecclesiastical authority, Catholic institutions should not consider themselves removed from those relationships with the hierarchical structures of the Church which must characterize institutions that call themselves Catholic.[20] A clear point of difference with the Land O' Lakes statement!

Ten years later, the revised 1983 Code of Canon Law,[21] also mandated by Pope John XXIII, along with the Second Vatican Council at the beginning of his papacy in 1959, introduced specific legislation intended to address all Catholic colleges and universities, those canonically dependent upon the Church as well as others that claimed a Catholic foundation, character, and purpose but which lacked an explicit canonical establishment. Pope John Paul II had already addressed the former type of institution before the new Code appeared in his apostolic constitution *Sapientia Christiana* (April 15, 1979).[22] It should be noted that the overwhelming majority of Catholic universities and colleges in the United States were of the latter variety. Needless to say, the provisions of the new Code received a chilly reception within the American Catholic academic community: again, it was "the winter of our discontent."

Himself a Catholic university professor, Pope John Paul II evidenced a great concern for Catholic institutions of higher learning. Following on the heels of both *Sapientia Christiana* and the 1983 Code of Canon Law, the Holy Father published a second apostolic constitution in 1990 intended to address Catholic universities and colleges that were not ecclesiastical in nature. *Ex Corde Ecclesiae* (August 15, 1990) was, in my opinion, the beginning of the "great thaw" in "the winter of our discontent."

While not original in the sense that they first appeared in a 1972 document "The Catholic University in the Modern World," produced by the Second International Congress of Delegates of Catholic Universities referred to earlier, the observations of Pope John Paul II summarized what he considered the "bottom line" for Catholic institutions of higher learning. These "essential characteristics" are particularly significant, not only because the Holy Father made them his own in *Ex Corde Ecclesiae,* but also because they are, themselves, the reflections of a body of international Catholic educators that helped make the case for a strengthening of the meaning of Catholic identity in Catholic post-secondary academic institutions. Pope John Paul II wrote that:

> Since the objective of a Catholic university is to assure in an institutional manner a Christian presence in the university world confronting the great problems of society and culture, every Catholic university as *Catholic*, must have the following *essential characteristics*:
>
> 1. Christian inspiration not only of individuals but of the university community as such;
>
> 2. A continuing reflection in the light of the Catholic faith upon the growing treasury of human knowledge, to which it seeks to contribute by its own research;
>
> 3. Fidelity to the Christian message as it comes to us through the Church;
>
> 4. An institutional commitment to the service of the people of God and of the human family in their pilgrimage to the transcendent goal which gives meaning to life.[23]

To assist in providing that assurance, the Holy Father noted, perhaps in part an answer to "Land O' Lakes" and other responses of similar kind:

> .   Every Catholic University, without ceasing to be a university, has a relationship to the Church that is essential to its institutional identity. . . . One consequence of its essential relationship to the Church is that the institutional fidelity of the university to the Christian message includes a recognition of and adherence to the teaching authority of the Church in matters of faith and morals. Catholic members of the university community are also called to a personal fidelity to the Church with all that this implies. Non-

Catholic members are required to respect the Catholic character of the university, while the university in turn respects
their religious liberty.[24]

The "new springtime" was on the horizon, but not without a "last
blast of winter"!

With the deftness and insight that have characterized his pontificate and all his writings, and drawing upon extraordinary human
experiences including that of being a university professor, Pope John
Paul II provided in *Ex Corde Ecclesiae* a *"magna carta"*[25] for
Catholic higher education throughout the Church, including the
United States. Calling for a clearly recognizable relationship
between Catholic colleges and universities, and the universal and
local church in which they exist,[26] the Holy Father has wisely
required that these institutions "operationalize" their Catholic identity through the assistance of a formal, juridical association with the
Church. This juridical dimension and its accompanying call for
greater accountability to the Church, unfortunately for some, dominated the discussions that would follow within the American
Catholic academic community. I say "unfortunately" because the
text and substance of the Holy Father's apostolic constitution – recognized by many, including those outside of the Catholic academic
community, as a magnificent exposition of the unique mission of
Catholic higher education – have often been reduced by some to a
mere set of legal norms.

When the constitution appeared in its final form, after three
drafts, and after the widest, most extensive public consultations ever
to accompany any Church document, it was generally well received
in America. Bishops and Catholic educators in the United States
appeared appreciative of the opportunities afforded them by the
Congregation for Catholic Education to be involved in its formulation. Some hesitation still lingered in these and other circles with
respect to the idea of any juridical norms at all – general or particular – but the prevailing sentiment seemed to be that "there was little
to cause anxiety and much to enable and inspire" those involved in
Catholic higher education.[27]

For the better part of the past twelve years, the bishops and the
Catholic academic community in the United States have been
engaged in a dialogue regarding the regional application or imple-

mentation of the constitution required in its "General Norms." Here again, several drafts and extensive consultations have accompanied the entire process.

From the beginning, two important presuppositions regarding the outcome of the process have been present: (1) that the application document would include juridical norms; (2) that the application document would be the product of the National Conference of Catholic Bishops or NCCB (now, the United States Conference of Catholic Bishops, or USCCB) as an episcopal document. Although these "understandings" were present, their implications were not always clearly appreciated, even among the bishops. One could legitimately claim that they were often avoided or ignored in the hopes they would simply "go away." In the months immediately preceding the 1999 NCCB meeting, these elements seemed to be all but forgotten, especially within Catholic academic circles. Discussions among Catholic university presidents at which I was present were openly hostile to the idea of episcopal juridical implementation.

The NCCB established an Implementation Committee of bishops in 1991, and several Catholic university presidents were invited to participate as consultors to the committee. An application document was developed, circulated for consultation, revised, approved by the NCCB with a vote of 224-6 on November 16, 1996 and forwarded to the Holy See for the *recognitio* required by canon law.[28] The Congregation for Catholic Education praised the application but indicated that it needed further juridic refinement, especially with respect to canon 812's provision regarding the mandate to teach theological disciplines, before it could be passed on to the Congregation for Bishops. Although the Holy See's critique was not well received in the United States, the NCCB Implementation Committee set out to respond positively to the Vatican request. A subcommittee was created in 1997, and revised drafts of an application document were developed and circulated in 1998 and 1999 respectively, again accompanied by extensive consultations. A strong argument was made in the Catholic and secular press by critics of the application, including several university presidents and even some bishops, that its provisions would yield "disastrous" results for Catholic universities and colleges in the United States if approved. Concerns were voiced that the new text was, at best, risky and, at worst, destructive of whatever progress had been made in the on-going dialogue about

Catholic identity that had been occurring among bishops and Catholic educators since *Ex Corde Ecclesiae* was first issued in 1990.

Anyone participating in American Catholic academic life since the Code of Canon Law was revised and promulgated in 1983 has heard these concerns before. In fact, some of the more controversial elements now found in the document of implementation known as "the Application"[29] are already contained in canon law's treatment of "Catholic Universities and Other Institutes of Higher Studies (cc. 807–814)," although they were deemed by educators and some canonists as doubtfully applicable in the American Catholic academic context. Similarly, as *Ex Corde Ecclesiae* progressed through its own draft stages in the late 1980s, these same concerns surfaced again.

It would be a mistake to separate "the Application" as it currently exists from the apostolic constitution itself. The "General Norms" accompanying *Ex Corde Ecclesiae* require "local and regional" implementation of the constitution.[30] A very concerted effort was made by those concerned with drafting "the Application" to insure that this text remained directly focused on the constitution, its exhortations, and its canonical provisions. In fact, several Catholic university presidents explicitly made that recommendation, myself included, during the consultation. Hence, what is required as normative in the resulting juridic text must always be viewed through the broader lens of the constitution itself for accurate interpretation and implementation.

It would equally be a mistake to separate the apostolic constitution and "the Application" from "the teaching of Vatican II and the directives of the Code of Canon Law" upon which it is based, as Pope John Paul II himself has stated.[31] *Ex Corde Ecclesiae*, he wrote, "was enriched by the long and fruitful experience of the Church in the realm of universities and open to the promise of future achievements that will require courageous creativity and rigorous fidelity."[32] In the minds of some, these two concepts – courageous creativity and rigorous fidelity – can make strange, even difficult bedfellows. I certainly do not believe that to be the case.

Apart from a few members of a vanishing generation of Catholic academics, there has been no revolt as had been predicted. In fact, Catholic institutions of higher learning in this country have been unusually quiet given recent history. Catholic universities and colleges continue to possess what the Church has called a "rightful" autonomy and a "legitimate" academic freedom. There have been no major legal battles, as had been predicted; and the allegedly adverse financial consequences have been exposed as myths. We have witnessed no "pastoral disaster," as one bishop claimed, or anything even slightly problematic. And Catholic teaching continues to be faithfully presented in our institutions by those who are faithful, although it is still challenged by some who view faith and reason at odds. I doubt very much that we will ever make converts of them, no matter what is said or done. The rigorous fidelity of their peers, a new generation of creative Catholic intellectuals and students seeking the truth, and, ultimately, time itself will work together toward the long hoped for renewal in Catholic higher education. The greatest evidence of renewal, however, is present on our campuses within the Catholic students themselves. It has been my experience that they are eager for leadership, hungry for truth, seeking to pray, and open to service to their neighbors. In many ways, they are teaching us.

Seasons do change. Winter gives way to spring. *Ex Corde Ecclesiae*, "the Application," and the "Guidelines concerning the Academic Mandatum in Catholic Universities (Canon 812)" promulgated to implement it, in my opinion, have spearheaded and inspired an attempt to present a coherent vision that continues to unfold for and within our Catholic universities and colleges in this country as a "new springtime" for Catholic higher education. It is up to all of us to replace the tired, negative rhetoric of the not so distant past when political and polarized ideologies created the "winter of our discontent" with "voices for a new springtime:" voices of Catholic scholars who are faithful; voices of Catholic scholars who are "convinced of the priority of the ethical over the technical, of the primacy of the person over things, of the superiority of the spirit over matter," joining knowledge to conscience;[33] voices that create a true fellowship of Catholic scholars who do not, in the words of our Holy Father's encyclical *Fides et Ratio*, "run from the truth as soon as they glimpse it because they are afraid of its demands,"[34] but who stand and serve the truth in charity.

The Very Reverend David M. O'Connell, C.M., J.C.D., is the fourteenth president of the Catholic University of America, and is the only member of the Congregation of the Mission to assume the presidency of the university in its 111-year history.

Having received his Licentiate ('87) and Doctorate ('90) in canon law from the Catholic University of America, Father O'Connell served as Dean of the College of Arts and Sciences and Associate Vice President of St. John's University in Jamaica, New York, and is also the recipient of the university's President's Medal. Father O'Connell also served as Academic Vice President of Niagara University.

A native of Philadelphia, Father O'Connell first became acquainted with the Vincentians at St. Joseph's College Preparatory School in Princeton, New Jersey, where he attended high school. He entered the Vincentians' College Seminary Program at Niagara University, where he combined studies in philosophy with performances in the university's theater program. The Vincentian novitiate and Theological Seminary in Northampton, Pennsylvania, prepared him for his ordination in 1982.

Notes

1   Reverend Thomas Dailey, o.s.f.s., "The Catholic Difference" in *Fellowship of Catholic Scholars Quarterly*, vol. 25, no. 2 (Spring 2002), p. 1.

2   Pope John Paul II, apostolic letter *Tertio Millennio Adveniente*, November 10, 1994 (Boston: Pauline Books and Media, 1994).

3   Pope John Paul II, apostolic letter *Novo Millennio Ineunte*, January 6, 2001 (Boston: Pauline Books and Media, 2001).

4   D. W. Brogan, *USA: An Outline of the Country, Its People and Institutions* (London, 1941), p.65, in John Tracy Ellis, "American Catholics and the Intellectual Life," *Thought* 30 (1955), p. 353 (hereinafter referred to as "Ellis").

5   Ellis, p. 353.

6   *Ibid.*, p. 354.

7   *Idem.*

8   See: C. Joseph Nuesse, *The Catholic University of America: A Centennial History* (Washington: CUA Press, 1990); see also: Margaret Mary Reher, "The Catholic University and Americanism: 1880–1900," in Margaret Mary Reher, *Catholic Intellectual Life in America: A History of Persons and Movements* (New York: Macmillan Publishing Company, Inc., 1989).

9   George Bull, "The Function of the Catholic Graduate School," *Thought* 13 (1938), p. 378.

10 Andrew M. Greeley, p.11, *From Backwater to Mainstream: A Profile of Catholic Higher Education,* Carnegie Commission Studies (New York: McGraw-Hill, 1969).

11 Pope John XXIII, apostolic constitution *Humanae Salutis,* December 25, 1961, in Walter M. Abbott, S.J., gen. ed., *The Documents of Vatican II* (New York: Guild Press, 1966), p. 703 (hereinafter referred to as "Abbott").

12 Pope John XXIII, "Opening Speech to the Council, October 11, 1962, in Abbott, p. 713.

13 Pope Pius XI, apostolic constitution *Deus Scientiarum Dominus,* May 24, 1931, in *Acta Apostolicae Sedis (AAS)* 23 (1931), p. 245.

14 G. Emmet Carter, "Education," in Abbott, p. 634.

15 Vatican Council II, Declaration on Christian Education, *Gravissimum educationis*, article 11 (October 28, 1965) in Abbott, p. 648.

16 International Federation of Catholic Universities, "Land O' Lakes Statement: The Nature of a Catholic University," Article 1 in Alice Gallin, O.S.U., ed., *American Catholic Higher Education: Essential Documents 1967–1990* (Notre Dame: University of Notre Dame Press, 1992), p. 7.

17 Pope Paul VI, encyclical *Humanae Vitae,* July 25, 1968 (Boston: Pauline Books and Media, 1968).

18 Delegates of the Second Congress of Catholic Universities of the World, "The Catholic University in the Modern World" in NCEA *College Bulletin* 35 (1973), pp. 1–10.

19 Pope John Paul II, apostolic constitution *Ex Corde Ecclesiae,* August 15, 1990 (Washington: United States Catholic Conference, 1990), hereinafter referred to as *"ECE."*

20 Cardinal Gabriel Marie Garrone, *"Litterae S. Cong. Pro Institutione Catholica Ad Rectores Universitatum Cath. Et Directores Institutionum Universit. Cath.,"* April 25, 1973 in *Periodica* 62 (1973), pp. 659–61.

21 Pope John Paul II, *The Code of Canon Law: Latin-English Edition* (Washington: The Canon Law Society of America, 1983).

22 Pope John Paul II, apostolic constitution *Sapientia Christiana*, April 15, 1979 (Washington: United States Catholic Conference, 1979).

23 *ECE,* I, Article 13, p. 13.

24 *Ibid.,* Article 27, pp. 22–23.

25 *Ibid.,* Article 8, p. 8.

26 *Ibid.,* Article 28, p. 23: "Bishops have a particular responsibility . . . to promote and assist in the preservation and strengthening of their Catholic identity. . . . Even when they do not enter directly into the internal governance of the university, bishops should not be seen as external agents but as participants in the life of the Catholic university."

27 Alice Gallin, o.s.u., ed., *American Catholic Higher Education: Essential Documents, 1967–1990* (Notre Dame: University of Notre Dame Press, 1992), p. 190.

28 Canon 455.2: The general degrees mentioned in paragraph 1 can be validly passed in a plenary session only if two-thirds of the members of the conference having a deliberate vote approve them; such decrees do not have binding force, unless they have been legitimately promulgated, after having been reviewed by the Apostolic See.

29 National Conference of Catholic Bishops, The Application of *Ex Corde Ecclesiae* for the United States (Washington: United States Catholic Conference, 2000).

30 *ECE*, II, Article 2, p. 37.

31 *Ibid.*, I, Article 11, p. 11.

32 *Ibid.*, I, Article 8, p. 9.

33 *Ibid.*, I, Article 18, p. 17.

34 John Paul II, encyclical *Fides et Ratio* ("Faith and Reason"), Vatican City: Libreria Editrice Vaticana, 1998), article 28, p. 44.

THE LIFE AND WORK OF THE CATHOLIC CHURCH IN THE 21ST CENTURY
Gregory Floyd

Introduction

I am delighted to be here at a conference entitled *Voices of the New Springtime.*

It's a wonderfully prophetic act to speak of the springtime when it doesn't feel like spring. But isn't it just like the Holy Father to speak of a new springtime when things are falling apart all around us, whether in the Church, the family, the board room, or the larger society? It's so audacious! He can speak of the new springtime, however, because he is the quintessential man of hope.

I would like to begin by honoring you who are gathered here for your faith, hope and love; for your Christ-like dedication; and for your cutting-edge work, especially in forming the minds of the young and of those men and women choosing priesthood and the religious life. It is a privilege to address you. It is important for me to state that up front to you as a group of theologians, scholars, and educators, because many Catholic CEOs (Chief Executive Officers) are profoundly upset about the state of Catholic education and their feelings will be reflected in my talk. You, however, are here because you are part of the solution and not part of the problem. You are part of the springtime of the intellectual life of the Church.

Let me set the stage for my talk with a bit of background information.

I am a married man. My wife Maureen and I have 9 children, ranging from 17 down to 2. In fact, three of our children are here with me. Our nine includes one child, John-Paul, who was killed in a car accident several years ago, and whose life and death were the inspiration for a book I wrote called *A Grief Unveiled.* I never intended to write a book, but I did want to give Maureen and the children a gift which would help them to see how the Lord led us through every parent's worst nightmare. We keep Johnny in the family roster because children theologize with effortless grace. "We have," they say, "a brother who lives in heaven."

I am the Northeast Director of Legatus, an international organization of Catholic CEOs and business owners. That means that my job is to get Legatus established in the Boston to Washington corridor. My wife and children and I are members of the People of Hope, a lay covenant community in northern New Jersey dedicated to prayer, evangelization, and family life. The community comprises some 700 people: families, singles, widows, divorced. The community has also been the matrix out of which two new religious communities were born: the Sisters of Jesus Our Hope in the diocese of Metuchen in New Jersey, and the Brotherhood of Hope in Boston. So, although for the moment we have lost our priests and sisters and other celibate members, we consider the fostering of priestly, religious, and celibate vocations central to our life as a lay community.

Prior to coming on board with Legatus, I was involved with two Catholic organizations dedicated to evangelization in a Catholic context: Fire Growth Resources and Renewal Resources. Through these organizations, we offered retreats and weekends that tried to help fellow Catholics to discover the riches of our tradition and to access the spiritual power that comes from conversion to Christ.

I directed that work for 15 years, during which we ran over 500 retreats. As we celebrated our 500th event, I sat before the Lord in the Blessed Sacrament and asked Him: "Would you like 500 more or do you have something else in mind?" At that point a friend of mine who was running Legatus asked me to consider working for the organization.

I mention these background pieces because evangelization, catechesis, and building Christian community come together in my work with Catholic CEOs, which is the focus of this talk.

What is Legatus?

One could begin this talk by asking the question: are there any heralds of the new springtime in the board rooms of corporate America? And the answer would be a resounding: Yes!

To expand upon that answer, let me tell you about the methodology I used. When I was asked to address this topic, I prayed about what angle might be helpful. What came to me was to use Legatus as a prism through which some of the forces of the new springtime at work in corporate America might be made visible. I decided to let the members of Legatus speak to you, in their own words. What you will hear, in a few minutes, is the collective voice of some 15 Catholic CEOs who personally communicated with me their views about the Church and business. Naturally, I do not claim to speak for all of Legatus, nor certainly for corporate America as a whole.

Before they speak, however, let me tell you something about the organization to which they belong, because, like so many other wonderful initiatives which have sprung up in the life of the church in the past few decades, I believe Legatus arose out an inspiration of the Holy Spirit.

"Legatus" is the Latin word for ambassador. The inspiration is taken from St. Paul's letter to the Corinthians: "You are ambassadors for Christ, Christ himself making appeal through you: be reconciled to God!"

At our December gala in New York two years ago, Cardinal Egan taught us that "legatus" means "publicist," as well. Legatus members are called to be ambassadors of Christ, but also to be His publicists in the marketplace.

Legatus is an organization of practicing Catholic CEOs, and heads of businesses, and their spouses. The spouse angle is important: in a milieu which tends to separate husbands and wives from each other, Legatus brings them together. Legatus was founded in 1986 by Tom Monaghan, the founder of Domino's Pizza and former owner of the Detroit Tigers. It is a lay organization with approximately 3000 members, representing about 1500 businesses in 50 chapters throughout the U.S. and Canada. The Legatus mission is to "study, live, and spread the faith in our business, professional, and personal lives."

This mission is accomplished in part by monthly meetings that include Mass, confession, dinner, and a talk. The talks focus on four key areas: faith, family, business, and modern culture. In these monthly meetings we have the opportunity to impart the social teaching of the Church to men and women who are actually running companies. These meetings also provide the environment in which CEOs can pray together, express their faith in the Lord, and discuss issues in their professional and family lives from a Catholic perspective.

They also have the opportunity to explore issues with first-rate speakers and join in genuine dialogue with each other.

I call it our monthly three-hour mini retreat. Over and over again I've watched the same dynamic unfold: acquaintances become relationships and relationships become friendships. This is good for business and good for the Church!

The criteria for membership are that prospective members be Catholics in good standing and be the top person in their company. Generally, the company must have a full time staff of 30 and 3 to 5 million in annual dollar volume; or, in the case of financial institutions, 10 full time staff and 100 million in managed assets. This is important to remember when you hear them speak: these are extraordinarily accomplished and successful individuals running anywhere from three-million-dollar companies to multi-billion dollar companies.

The Members Speak.

The five questions I asked Legatus members to answer were these:

1. What is the relevance and value of Catholicism as a herald in the world of business in the 21st century?

2. What can the Church contribute to corporate life (here I mean Church in the broadest and most universal sense)?

3. What is the Church's specific contribution to you as a business leader?

4. What does it mean to be a faithful Catholic in the corporate world?

5. What specific contributions can you as Catholic business leaders offer the Church?

In answering these five questions, I have organized their responses and taken on their collective persona in order to give voice to their thoughts, hopes and concerns.

1. *What is the relevance and value of Catholicism as a herald in the world of business in the 21st century?*

The relevance of Catholicism as a herald in the world of business is not what it could be or should be. The real question is: "Are

Catholics *willing* to make their Catholicism relevant? I don't think so. Are Catholics *willing* to be ambassadors for their faith and marshal combatants to turn the tide of secular humanism? Are we *willing* to make these moral and ethical issues important in an age when one shouldn't be "judgmental?"

Catholics in the world of business are often at best mere shadows, fearful that they might rock the boat, be on the wrong side of the issue and have their promotions thwarted for being considered right wing religious zealots. Add to the mix the Catholic divorce lawyers who profit in the seedy trade of destroying families, the Catholic politicians who vote "pro-choice," and the business people who trade and do business with clients in direct opposition to the teachings of the Church.

Plug in what's "relevant" in music, films and television and one has to ask: "Is there anyone or anything out there that can turn the tide of *what has become* relevant to *what should be* relevant?"

Nevertheless, the world of business and commerce will define the economic environment in which most people in the United States will live and work in the 21st century. The Church must recognize this reality. The Church must assume a leadership role in defining the true meaning of a capitalist society, and not leave it to others who would exploit the opportunities for purely personal gain. As Michael Novak says in *The Catholic Ethic and Spirit of Capitalism*: "The defining characteristic of a capitalist economy is neither the free market nor incentives nor profit. All are pre-conditions. Capitalism does not come into existence until institutions are established that systematically support and nourish the creative capacities of human beings to invent, to discover, and to practice the fundamental human right to innovate."

Catholic men and women are called to carry Jesus' message to the marketplace. Indeed we are called to be apostles to a diverse and scattered community. In our country this community of business persons is characterized by God-given entrepreneurial juices, a desire to succeed, build, achieve, create, and, as a result, to reap profits and increase wealth. People of all economic circumstances are driven by many of these same desires, though it might at times seem otherwise.

These are reasonable goals, often disparaged and denigrated by those in academia and the Church hierarchy. However, the opportunity to put into practice the Gospel way of life in a concrete and tangible way is present in the marketplace to a greater degree than we commonly think. More than any other group, Catholic business leaders are in a unique position to implement and put into practice Christ's principles of ownership and labor so clearly enunciated in the encyclicals *Rerum Novarum, Quadragesimo Anno* and *Centesimus Annus.* Because so much of our culture is based on our economy, which is ultimately based on businesses, it is imperative that we in the corporate world live out our faith in a clearer way if society is to live up to its potential.

How do we do this? Our faith guides us to be moral. Honest. Caring. The Holy Father exhorts us to understand business as an occasion for virtue. How? By discovering and implementing the many different ways it serves and satisfies the human needs of those with whom we have contact. The Church has pointed out that the greatest contribution of business is to provide work for people. This honest work translates into a fair wage enabling people to raise families, provide benefits, give people a sense of their own dignity, and work for the common good. The value of Catholicism as a herald in the world of business today is that it calls us as men and women to be committed to some simple truths.

There is a God to whom we are bound in life and death. Our bonds to each other form a life-long obligation to grow in awareness and love. It matters enormously that we live our lives in the spirit of knowing, loving and serving God. Given this, Catholics, be they laity, religious or ordained, must practice what they preach. As business leaders, we must also warn and fight against the dehumanizing and unjust effects of unrestricted capitalism. The recent events in the United States regarding senior executives of major public companies demonstrates the danger, and the evil, of trusting an economic model without regard to justice, proper stewardship, honesty and social welfare.

The Church has spoken out on these issues, but she needs to do so more forcefully and regularly. The Church can add value and impact in these areas, and the leadership of the Church as well as Catholic leaders in business, must step forward in word and in deed to ensure that the light of Christ shine above all others. I would add that because of the scandals among some U.S. clergy, and the publicity surrounding these scandals, the ability of the Church hierarchy in the States to speak from a position of moral leadership is not very strong at the moment. This argues for lay leaders, more than ever before, to take the lead. The voice of the Church needs to be heard!

2. *What can the Church contribute to corporate life?*

One of the first things the Church can contribute to corporate life is to continue to be what she is and to live the teachings that she professes. The Church must reclaim her educational institutions. She will never contribute to corporate life by giving diplomas to our youth while:

- Giving honorary doctorates to pro-abortion advocates;

- Featuring enemies of the Church as speakers and lecturers under the guise of the first amendment;

- Removing crucifixes so as not to offend anyone, when no one asked that crucifixes be removed;

- Prohibiting strong Catholic programs on Catholic campuses.

She will never contribute to corporate life while pro-life programs are not supported by our bishops, priests, and university leaders. If we can't teach the truth to our young impressionable students when they are in our charge at the high school, college, and university levels, then how can one even conceive that the Church can contribute to corporate life later on? It won't happen unless we start with the young. The Holy Father doesn't preach to the corporate world, he holds World Youth Days!

But the Church *can* be an active partner in our efforts to educate young people about issues of faith and reason. College students arrive with a very meager understanding of their faith. The Church can and must be the beacon of honesty and truth. Church leaders need to be visible to our young people during the last formal opportunity we have to help them build their faith. Why? *Because the Church often forms the consciences of individuals who end up in the business world.* The Church can bring the Eucharist to corporate life! The Church can reach out to young businessmen and women with initiatives that are faith-based. Catholic education has failed miserably in this area. Catholic colleges maintain contact with their alumni primarily in order to get their money. What do Catholic colleges do to save the souls of their alumni? I'll tell you: virtually nothing! Oh yes, they do tell you about the Mass they have on campus, but it's only once a year. Yet the possibilities here are limited only by our imaginations.

The Church can clearly define the high principles upon which the free market rests. The Church should emphasize the bedrock need for a growing economy to provide the jobs and opportunities for individuals to take proper care of their families and achieve satisfaction from gainful employment.

The Church could certainly improve upon her portrayal of business as a calling. The art of producing goods and services is sometimes portrayed as a vulgar activity. But business persons are called to be God's co-creators in the economic realm. The Church should recognize this role and affirm it.

The Church must also continue to speak out on topics relevant to business and business people. Why not have a periodic global summit of Church and business leaders to focus on particular topics? By including highly visible business leaders, several good things would happen:

First, the event would garner a lot of attention (take note of other such gatherings that have included people like George Soros and Bill Gates: the media loves these types of events!).

Secondly, these business leaders would be professing their Catholicism, which is a good message to send to the world.

Third, there would be communiqués from Church and business leaders together, which would have more of an impact than either group doing it on its own.

The bottom line is this: business people desperately need the Church's help in putting their faith to work in their work lives.

3. *What is the Church's specific contribution to you as a business leader?*

The Church is my home. I feel a void if I am not able to attend Mass before going to work. The Church provides me with the opportunity to receive Holy Communion so that I can more directly bring Christ into my work life. The sacraments, especially the Eucharist, are a source of strength, protection and encouragement that drives the engine of my professional life. I try to view all my business decisions, especially those affecting people, in the light of Jesus' teachings and the popes' encyclicals. The Church gives me guidance in my ethical reflections and difficult decisions.

The Church stands against secular humanism. She defines truth and provides a moral compass for me to help me live and work as a business leader. The Church is the voice of moral authority and a support system for my vocation in the workplace. Through her teaching and pronouncements, the Church calls me on. The simplicity of that call is expressed in the Beatitudes and in the corporal works of mercy. These are a daily challenge to me. My faith calls me to live in service to others, especially the "least of the brethren." I am called by the Church to walk the walk and not just talk the talk.

4. *What does it mean to be a faithful Catholic in the corporate world?*

It means many things. I think it means to work hard every day to understand what God wants from me in my work life, and to do as Jesus has taught me to do in dealing with my employees, colleagues, customers and others. It means that my Catholicism is visible for other to see, and that I should be ready and willing to discuss my beliefs with anyone. It means that I act in a way that is consistent with the ideals of justice, compassion and kindness. It means being willing to take a hit if I have to make a call that may not be perceived as being the best for the company, but is consistent with my beliefs.

I t means to know, love and serve God *in this world* and to ask Him to intercede in all my daily thoughts so that I may draw others to Him and create in them a desire to be better. It means to quietly and humbly ask God to direct all my actions for His greater good. It means to have uncompromising faith in His divine providence and to trust that the gates of hell will not prevail against His will. It means to seek business solutions for the good of all involved and not for the profit of a few; to stand up for my beliefs; to quietly but strongly practice the virtues of my faith.

It means that I must ensure that employees receive a just wage sufficient to support their families and provide for their future; and that I provide the opportunities for them to grow as employees and as human persons. It means treating all with patience, love and respect. It means running a sound, healthy and profitable business so that those who depend on it for their livelihood can work in employment security.

It means I must give witness to Jesus by the example of my life. It means I must faithfully and honestly practice my Catholic Christian beliefs in all circumstances. It means remaining faithful to the magisterium even when popular culture and the media would lead me elsewhere. It means that I cannot compromise the principles of integrity and faithfulness for profit or illicit gain.

5. *What specific contributions can you as a business leader offer the Church?*

We can do a lot more than offer financial support to the Church, which is often all we are called upon to do. As business leaders we can bring an economic viewpoint to the Church's social endeavors. We can help provide insights to the long-term effects that government and Church policies have on job creation.

We can also bring our unique perspective to Catholic higher education. We could, for example, offer courses on the great labor encyclicals. We could offer courses on the Christian philosophy of · the market economy. Intellectuals sometimes overlook the self-reforming capacities of capitalism. We can offer pragmatic, down-to-earth, realistic, action-oriented approaches to problems and problem-solving.

We can live a visibly Christian life in the business world. To the extent that being a business leader results in material rewards, we can share generously in the spirit of the Gospel. Whatever gifts we have been given that have made us successful in business can be put to use directly for the Church.

We can offer management skills. Consider that the Church hierarchy is, on one level, in leadership roles much like CEO's. Much of what we are experiencing today reflects poor management. Avoidance of scandal was made primary; short-term solutions to ongoing problems became the norm. Much of this is the result of our very human natures! When CEOs act in such a way, inevitably disaster, both corporate and personal, follows. Stark examples of the above abound in the church and society.

We can offer the Church models of how to successfully manage the secular issues it often faces, whether structural, financial or on the level of perception. Corporations and their leaders have learned that the media can be both a friend and a foe in times of crisis . . . especially post-Tylenol. The fact that communications are crafted does not mean that they are a prevarication. *Communications must be molded to resonate with the experience and vernacular of the audience.* Business leaders can and should contribute their expertise in this area to the Church.

We can challenge other Catholics to get involved, to protect our rights as Catholics, to demand excellence from our colleges and universities (and boycott those who do not wish to proclaim themselves Catholic).

We can bring a joyful, prayerful attitude to the workplace. We can be different. We can bring Jesus with us everywhere. We can learn to love and not to judge. We can be in the world but not of it.

Conclusion

These are the voices, distilled into a common voice, of corporate CEOs and business owners who live their faith in the marketplace. Do they sound like preachers, catechists, evangelists, and apologists? They are. And they're running profitable businesses. And they're raising families and serving in their communities. But most fundamentally, they are disciples and witnesses, witnesses to what they have seen and heard and touched – the Word who is Life (1 John). They are just a few voices from the chorus of Legatus, and Legatus is just one little room in the Father's house.

I don't have time to tell you of the innumerable personal acts of justice and charity that these men and women perform, but they are a moving testimony to grace in action. The Holy Father reminds us that work is the key to the social question. There is no celebration of destitution in the Bible, of material poverty per se. As one CEO said, "My preferential option for the poor is to get them out of poverty." A CEO can do a lot, not only in the material realm but also in transforming the ethos of the workplace. We must remember, as a professor of mine once said, that no dimension of creation is cordoned off from God's care and concern.

My suggestion: Get some of these people on your boards! Get them teaching at your colleges and seminaries! Get them training your priests and seminarians in some of the areas in which they are so magnificently gifted. Better yet, have them take over some of those areas so you can preach Christ in season and out. I know they want to serve whatever is authentically Catholic.

And, on the other hand, they need you:

- Bringing them knowledge of the truth;
- Filling in the gaps in their catechesis;
- Giving them the broader and deeper perspective that the discipline and study provide.

The psalmist cries out: "Behold how good and pleasant it is when brethren dwell in unity (Ps 133:1). It occurred to me last night, while reflecting on this talk, that in the springtime, *all* creation comes alive, so to speak. There is a unity in that. May we be part of that marvelous Catholic unity. May we all work together, to announce in word and deed, in all the academic, cultural, artistic, business, professional, and political corridors to which the Holy Spirit gives us access, the magnificent words of St. Paul: "Let all proclaim to the glory of the Father that Jesus Christ is Lord (Phil 2:11)."

Gregory Floyd is the Northeast Regional Director of Legatus. Founded by Thomas Monaghan, Legatus is the only organization in the world designed exclusively for top-ranking Catholic business leaders. The organization currently has over 1,400 members in 44 chapters across the United States and internationally on three continents. Legatus is the conduit connecting two powerful realities, the challenge of top-tier business leadership, and the most profound and convincing body of religious knowledge in the history of human thought. Legatus seeks to translate the teachings of Christ and the social teaching of the Church into practical applications for our members so that they can spread the faith through good example, good deeds, and high ethical standards.

Gregory Floyd is also the author of *A Grief Unveiled: One Father's Journey Through the Death of a Child*, which has become one of the best-selling books of the Paraclete Press. Mr. Floyd is also the composer of an album of songs entitled *Angel in Disguise*.

Mr. Floyd is also a leader in the People of Hope, a Catholic community of some 700 people in New Jersey. He has also served on the community's outreach teams in England and Ireland. Gregory and his wife Maureen are the parents of nine children from seventeen down to two.

FIDES ET RATIO:
A CONTEXT FOR DEVELOPING
THE NEW FEMINISM
Pia Francesca de Solenni

I.

Some have suggested that John Paul II will be known as John Paul the Great after his death. It makes sense. He has gone where no pope has gone before, both theologically and geographically. Within the parameters of theology, he has seen fit to discuss the most contemporary issues, including feminism and sex. To a certain extent, we have become accustomed to his various discourses on these issues, particularly those concerning the dignity and vocation of woman. I sometimes wonder if these obvious discourses were simply laying the groundwork for something more intricate, something that takes the obvious to a level we have not experienced? After years of teaching on the dignity of woman, his most striking comment is found at the end of an encyclical that apparently has little to do with the feminine vocation: *Fides et Ratio*. He concludes his thorough discussion on the relationship between philosophy and theology with his customary invocation of the Blessed Virgin Mary. This comes as no surprise to anyone who is familiar with his writings. His conclusion, however, goes beyond the standard invocation. He finishes his discussion of the two wings, i.e., philosophy and theology, by extolling Mary as the paradigm of philosophers:

> I turn in the end to the woman whom the prayer of the Church invokes as *Seat of Wisdom*, and whose life itself is a true parable illuminating the reflection contained in these pages. For between the vocation of the Blessed Virgin and the vocation of true philosophy, there is a deep harmony. Just as the Virgin was called to offer herself entirely as human being and as woman that God's Word might take flesh and come among us, so too philosophy is called to

offer its rational and critical resources that theology, as the understanding of faith, may be fruitful and creative. And just as in giving her assent to Gabriel's word, Mary lost nothing of her true humanity and freedom, so too when philosophy heeds the summons of the Gospel's truth its autonomy is in no way impaired. Indeed, it is then that philosophy sees all its enquiries rise to their highest expression. This was a truth which the holy monks of Christian antiquity understood well when they called Mary "the table at which faith sits in thought."[1] In her they saw a lucid image of true philosophy and they were convinced of the need to *philosophari in Maria*.[2]

After a first reading of the encyclical, this closing thought suggests that the text be re-read in light of the Holy Father's exposition of the vocation of woman, a prominent theme throughout his pontificate.

Another key aspect of *Fides et Ratio* is the emphasis on Aquinas. In addition to the various citations of the Angelic Doctor's work, the Holy Father insists upon the important role of this work in philosophy. First he cites Leo XIII: "Just when Saint Thomas distinguishes perfectly between faith and reason, he unites them in bonds of mutual friendship, conceding to each its specific rights and to each its specific dignity."[3] With this framework in mind, as if to both underscore and to give a fatherly reprimand, the Pope writes:

> If it has been necessary from time to time to intervene on this question, to reiterate the value of the Angelic Doctor's insights and insist on the study of his thought, this has been because the magisterium's directives have not always been followed with the readiness one would wish. In the years after the Second Vatican Council, many Catholic faculties were in some ways impoverished by a diminished sense of the importance of the study not just of Scholastic philosophy but more generally of the study of philosophy itself. I cannot fail to note with surprise and displeasure that this lack of interest in the study of philosophy is shared by not a few theologians.[4]

Although the Holy Father introduces this in the fourth chapter of the encyclical, it helps to bring it forth so as to better develop an understanding of the encyclical as a whole. Immediately after introducing the subject of the encyclical, the Pope turns to the discussion of the most fundamental relationship, i.e. the relationship between God and his Church. He turns first to the Church. She is the bearer of a message originating in God.[5] While she bears the message, it is Jesus who reveals it.[6] This relationship of the bearer and the revealer is based on definite notions of femininity and masculinity, namely bride and groom, which is the relationship of God to his people.

The spousal relationship describes the most intimate unions: the Church and Christ, the soul and God, husband and wife. These unions are based not so much on sameness as on difference and complementarity. At the risk of oversimplifying, the partners fit together like two pieces of a puzzle. If we were to take two pieces exactly alike, they would not fit together as one. The underlying notion of the spousal relationship helps us to understand difference as a creative and complimentary element.

God, in revealing himself, manifests that he is a loving God who wants to make himself known to his creatures and who invites them to enter into a reciprocal, loving relationship. The act of revealing corresponds to his being both groom and father. Generally speaking, men love according to the fruits of their labor. Men love when they protect, they love when they build environment, and they love when they have an object to protect and for which to build an environment.

Analogously, when God reveals, he makes himself known. Those to whom God has revealed himself are given a particular identity as knowers of God. They *receive* his revelation. Revelation is directed to them as to an end and a purpose, they become a chosen people. When he reveals himself, God creates an intimate bond of knowledge with his people. This bond exists in a two-fold manner: between God and his people and between the people themselves. This creates an environment in which the Church exists. The Church has both a relationship to God as bride and a relationship among those who make up the Church. Once the bond has been created, God must protect his bride so that the revelation is carried on and not corrupted. Hence, we have a structured and infallible Church.

The Church, although made up of both men and women, is essentially feminine. Mary the mother of God fully realizes and expresses "the very essence of the Church as a community consecrated with the integrity of a '*virgin*' heart to become the '*bride*' of Christ and '*mother*' of believers."[7] Since the Pope sees her as the paradigm of philosophers, it is worthwhile exploring this development in "the feminine genius,"[8] which he expects to produce "new and surprising manifestations" in the Third Millennium.

Understanding the spousal (and gender influenced) relation of Jesus to the Church gives form to our understanding of the Church as feminine, and enables us to continue our quest to better understand femininity so that we will therefore become a better Church and bride. Despite the rationalistic tendencies of the recent centuries, it should come as no surprise to us that there exists a feminine aspect of philosophy and knowing. Throughout Scripture, wisdom is personified as a woman. The man in search of her pursues her as a lover.[9] When he possesses her, he stays close to her and entrusts his children to her, as a wife and mother. His possession in no way resembles servitude. If anything, he is beholden to her: ". . . he dwells in the shade of her glory."[10]

Mary further exemplifies the philosopher when we look at the "basic rules" that the Holy Father sets forth for acquiring deeper knowledge:

1. Reason must realize that human knowledge is a journey which allows no rest.

2. Such a path is not for the proud who think that everything is the fruit of personal conquest.

3. One must be grounded in the "fear of God" whose transcendent sovereignty and provident love in the governance of the world reason must recognize.[11]

If we reverse these rules, we can see them played out in the annunciation and the visitation.[12] Recall that before Gabriel appeared to Mary, he appeared to Zacarias. Zacarias's response to the message, indeed to the revelation, was that it simply could not be. In a sense, he closed his ears to the message and refused to hear. In response, God closed his mouth by making him mute. Zacarias's assent is not manifested until, literally, the infant is deposited in his lap. At this point, he articulates his acceptance by giving the infant his name: John. With this, he regains the ability to speak.

Mary gets the same messenger and an even greater message. She, too, questions how this can be. Gabriel explains and at the same time gives her the message he gave to Zacarias. Mary answers with her *fiat:* "Behold the handmaid of the Lord; let it be done unto me according to thy word." Within this scenario of the annunciation, we see the third and part of the second rule played out.

Upon hearing the news of Elizabeth's pregnancy and, more importantly, assenting to the Incarnation, Mary begins "the journey that knows no rest" and the second rule: the journey of the messenger. She carries what is revealed to her and bears that knowledge. She travels to assist Elizabeth. Thus, she begins her journey as a messenger which is first recognized by the infant John *in utero*. Upon Elizabeth's recognition of the message, Mary replies with her *Magnificat*, thereby further illustrating the second rule. As she carries the message along the journey, she comes to know it better and better, until they arrive together at Golgotha.

II.

In *Fides et Ratio*, the Holy Father defines the human person as the "one who seeks truth".[13] The task and nobility of man and woman lies in exploring truth with their reason.[14] This is reminiscent of Aquinas (and others), who explains that the human vocation is to know, ultimately to know God.[15] It is not a vain quest. Rather, it is the work of a lifetime, which men and women have been given to do together. Aquinas understood this and the pope reiterates it when he writes that we are not created to live alone and that learning involves an interpersonal relationship.[16]

The crisis of philosophy goes beyond its mere distinction from theology. It has in fact been isolated, and within that isolation; it has become rationalistic and self-determining. Since at least the time of Descartes, the receptive process has been left out of philosophy. Modern philosophy has emphasized the active aspects of the mind so that knowing has lost its receptive element of receiving truth and reality, of conforming to objective truth. It has lost any sense of the feminine.[17] We see the antithesis of this in Mary at the Annunciation. She receives truth and reality. She conforms to objective truth even when she does not fully understand it. Many would say that she was "taken in," but we know that her response is not an unknowing response.

To understand the role of Mary and, hence, the feminine aspect of philosophy, we turn to the thought of Aquinas. Aquinas explains that in the mind, there is no difference between the sexes. The mind is the same for man and woman.[18] Knowing is a process which also involves the body because all human knowledge begins with sense experience; so it involves our entire being: body and soul. The soul is the form of the body, it makes the body human.[19] The soul is the intellective part, but it is informed through the senses, i.e., through the body. In this way the soul and body are intricately united. Epistemology is, therefore, central to Aquinas's consideration of human nature and its activity because it is the study of the activity that belongs to each of us as a composite of body and soul. Knowing exists for the knower and it requires the use of the knower's capabilities.

For Aquinas, the object of knowledge will retain some characteristic of the subject because everything comes to be known in a way that is particular to each subject.[20] Therefore, humans know in one way, and angels know in another, because they are different types of subjects. If we continue this line of thought, we realize that although all human subjects share the same nature, there is something particular in the way that each human subject knows specifically.[21] From our experience we know that, given varying intellectual capabilities, individual men and women will know the same thing in different ways.

When discussing the human cognitive power, Aquinas uses several terms: *mens, intellectus*, and *ratio*.[22] He tends to use *mens* and *intellectus* (mind and intellect) interchangeably and *intellectus* and *ratio* (intellect and reason) interchangeably. For example, in his discussion of the *imago Dei* found in man and woman, Aquinas uses *mens* and *intellectus* interchangeably to name the same faculty.[23] Aquinas uses *intellectus* as a sort of middle term and gives it two meanings. When discussing the power or potency of the human soul, he uses *mens* and *intellectus*. When discussing the act of this power, he uses *intellectus* and *ratio*. Because the second set of terms refers to a human act, they also entail a passage of time. The human soul does not simply know but it comes to know. Once the human being comes to know, the act of knowing is fixed within the boundaries of time. The act of knowing is constantly subject to cessation insofar as, at any moment, the subject might cease to actively know what it presently knows. The verbs *intelligere* and *ratiocinari* correspondingly describe the activity of the *intellectus* and *ratio* as the acts of the *mens* or *intellectus*. This coming to know (*intelligere*) is the act of the power or potency expressed by the first group of terms and it requires the element of time because the coming to know is neither innate nor immediate. We do not know immediately; it takes time for us to come to know, i.e., the process of going from not-knowing to knowing involves time. Even when we come to know, our knowing is wholly contingent and not independent.

In God, knowing or *intelligere* is the same as his being and, therefore, the same as his essence.[24] As humans, however, we can exist without *intelligere*, for example, as a sleeping newborn infant exists.[25] But the human being possesses the faculty of *intellectus* because this faculty is proper to the human being.[26] It is not the act of *mens*, or the act of knowing, which makes us human.[27]

We are the composite of body and soul; so, even if our intellectual powers are limited or stifled, we are still human and our soul still has the potentiality or disposition of a rational soul. Someone who exists in a vegetative state, for example, remains a human being. The child who cannot yet reason is still a human being. A mentally deficient or retarded person is still a human being. An inebriated person does not stop being a human being because *intellectus* or reason is impeded. Despite the imperfections of a human's cognitive powers, the human nonetheless remains fully human. So even though the intellect or the mind is not actualized, the essence of the soul is not altered. Someone with unactualized or extremely limited cognitive powers is still a human being. Because nothing of the nature of the human soul changes with regard to the actualization of *mens*, *mens* cannot be the essence of the soul. Rather, it is a power or capability of the human soul.

While *mens* is not the essence of the human soul, it is the most characteristic faculty of the human soul and, principally through it, the soul arrives at perfection.[28] For this reason, Aquinas nuances his discussion of the nature of *mens*. Generally speaking, there is a way in which *mens* is passive or receptive, it suffers, it receives both as *intellectus* and as *ratio*. Aquinas discusses the three uses of the verb to suffer (*pati*). The first is its most proper usage: when something is removed (*removetur*) from that which is fitting to itself, whether according to its nature or to its proper inclination.[29] Because it is fitting, it is something that is essentially good. The examples that Aquinas gives are of water losing its coolness by being heated and the case when someone becomes ill or is saddened (loses health or joy). (According to Aquinas's antiquated physics, it is proper to the nature of water to be cool. It is only made hot by some external force acting on it.)

Aquinas's example of sickness or sadness is particularly beautiful and striking because it implicitly manifests his human teleology. We are not created to be sick or sad. Health and happiness are proper to our nature and the things toward which we tend. Sickness and sadness are imperfections. The passage indicates that our end is something good and desirable.

The second sense of suffering is less proper and occurs when something is cast away (*abiicitur*) from the thing, whether suitable or unsuitable.[30] In this sense, one suffers when healed because the sickness is removed. Suffering is not limited to the consideration of pain. It plays a part in a larger consideration of being acted upon by another.

The third sense of suffering is when something receives what it is in potency to receive.[31] Something is added to it, something either good or bad. It is said to suffer *communiter*. Anything which passes from potency to act, therefore, suffers in the third sense, i.e., the most common type of suffering. The human is the least perfect of the intellectual beings because it does not know innately. Aristotle calls the human *intellectus* or *mens* a *tabula rasa* (blank tablet/clean slate) upon which nothing is written when it first comes into existence.[32] Aquinas's third sense of suffering stems from Aristotle's discussion in the *De Anima*.[33] *Intellectus* is potential because, until it knows even the smallest thing, it is not actualized. It is passive or receptive because it comes to know by receiving the forms of things as possessions. *Intellectus* keeps the intellectual forms which, in a sense, become part of it.[34] In this sense of becoming the object, *intellectus* suffers because it receives that which it was not and that which it did not previously have. It is acted upon and changed. Similarly, *ratio*, until it begins its discursive activity, is passive because its potency has not yet been actualized. The passive element is present, therefore, in both *intellectus* and *ratio*. Gilson explains, "Intellectual passivity is, then, a natural correlative of limitation of being."[35]

Intellectus passes from not knowing to knowing because it possesses an active part corresponding to the passive part, namely the agent intellect.[36] The agent intellect distinguishes the sensible things from the intelligible things, or abstracts the intelligible from the sensible, because material things can only produce a sensible likeness of themselves.[37] This sensible likeness, however, is not the immaterial likeness or form which is kept in the mind and, thus, imprinted on *intellectus*.

The agent intellect makes things intelligible to the human *mens*.[38] The effect caused by the sensible thing acting on the sensitive subject is a phantasm. The phantasm is the likeness of an individual thing received by or impressed upon the sensible organs.[39] Upon receiving the phantasm, *intellectus* has only a particular knowledge. It knows only that particular phantasm. In order to understand or know the phantasms which it receives, the agent intellect must separate what is particular from what is universal to the phantasm. In order to know the *quiddity* of a thing, *intellectus* must put together the nature of the thing with the particular thing itself. At first glance this seems to be a catch-22 because *intellectus* cannot know the nature of something without knowing particular things from which it has abstracted the universal.[40] By means of the phantasm, the agent intellect abstracts the form of the sensible object and in this way the form is imprinted upon and kept in *intellectus*. *Intellectus* both appraises the particular things and takes the universal from the particular things.

Intellectus considers being in general; this is its object.[41] Before we know what something is, we know that it is. Things which can be known have being and *intellectus* first apprehends being or existence.[42] The process of coming to know is that whereby *intellectus* comes to know more about the being of the object, i.e., it comes to know what type of being it is and not just that it is a being.

The motion from potency to act, from the *tabula rasa* to a detailed script is the third type of suffering (*quoddam pati*). Memory is the capacity to retain the sense impressions written upon the *tabula rasa*, but memory is not something separate from *intellectus* because memory is an operation of *intellectus* itself. There are two types of memory. One is internal sense memory. The other is intellectual memory. Within *intellectus* there can be only the passive *intellectus* and the agent *intellectus*. Intellectual memory falls into the realm of the passive *intellectus* because it receives.[43]

The memory, like *ratio*, is another aspect of *mens*; and it is the same faculty as the *intellectus*. The act of *intellectus* (*intelligere*) is the immediate and simple grasping of truth.[44] The act of *ratio* (*ratiocinari*) is a process of moving from one known thing to another known thing so as to arrive at truth which is intelligible or understandable.[45] The angels are pure intelligences. We, however, are the lowest in the order of intellectual beings and, therefore, our knowledge is not immediate like that of the angels. We begin with the more known in order to arrive at the knowledge of things which are less known, using both *ratiocinari* and *intelligere*.[46] The act of *intelligere* is simply more perfect than the act of *ratiocinari* because the end, i.e., knowing, is immediately obtained. *Ratiocinari* has an aspect of temporality because it is a process of coming to know which spans a duration of time. As Aquinas explains, there are some things which human *intellectus* does not naturally (immediately) know and it remains for *ratio* to arrive at them or to seek for them by means of *studio* or diligence.[47] But in order for *ratio* to arrive at knowledge, it must begin with knowledge of the particulars.

Knowledge of the particulars is primarily received through the senses. Before speaking of the intellective powers of the soul, Aquinas examines the lower powers of the animal soul, e.g., vegetative and generative. At the end of his consideration, he turns to the interior senses: common sense or the basic senses of sensation, imagination, the sentient power of judgment, and sensitive memory.[48] When the senses perceive something, the phantasm they receive is kept by the power of imagination. Aquinas calls the imagination a type of treasury or repository of forms received through the senses.[49]

Aquinas's discussion of the interior senses of the body brings to light an important consideration. The sensitive potencies are proper to the corporeal organs. Therefore, humans, by virtue of their bodies, are the only intellectual creatures that have the sensitive powers. The body is also the one thing which differentiates man and woman.

For Aquinas, man and woman admit no difference of soul or of mind. The difference lies in their respective physical bodies.[50] Although both man and woman have the same mind (*mens*) which is comprised of *ratio* and *intellectus*, they differ in their knowing according to the type of body through which they sense.[51] Every human senses through a different particular body, but men and women differ in the type of human body through which they sense. Aquinas's anthropology has already laid the basis for a complementarity between man and woman at the level of procreation and this implies that a complementarity must exist in the other work which they share, namely the work particular to them as intellectual creatures: knowing God. Since every aspect of knowing is the same, the way in which man and woman compliment each other in the work of knowing must be based on the sense knowledge received through their differentiated bodies.[52] Except for the difference in bodies, man and woman share the particular blend of active and receptive (or passive) powers in the *intellectus* and *ratio*.

For Plato, the body only entraps or contains the human soul and obstructs knowing or the process of coming to know. It does not have an essential role in this process. Aquinas, however, follows Aristotle's view that things come to be in the *intellectus* or mind as they are received through the senses of the body. Everything that man or woman comes to know ultimately has its basis in sense perception.[53] *Intellectus* receives the material, so to speak, for universals and knowledge from particular bodies which are perceived by the body. Although the body in a sense feeds data to the *intellectus*, it does not participate in the intellectual act per se. First, through the senses, *intellectus* perceives the being of a thing. Secondly, it perceives the essence of a particular corporeal being through the senses of the body. The agent intellect abstracts, i.e., it separates what is common to all the particulars so as to arrive at the universal which is the common element in all the particulars.[54]

Aquinas compares the relation of *ratio* to *intellectus* to the relation of motion to rest and to the relation of acquiring to having.[55] *Ratio* is intrinsically imperfect and, at the same time, absolutely necessary for human knowing. Rest and motion are not two different potencies, but two different aspects of the same thing. Similarly, *ratio* and *intellectus* are not two different potencies or powers. They are different ways and different degrees of perfection by which the intellective power works within the human soul. Reason proceeds from the terms received by the intellect. Intellect is the "repose of agreement at the beginning and at the end of its act of reasoning."[56]

Intellectus seeks to apprehend the form of the object because the form gives the essence of the object. Apprehending the form is not the same as separating the objects into their proper categories. Knowing (*intelligere*) requires more than simply apprehending the form. The first step in knowing is the sensing or awareness of being of the material body. This is the object impressed upon the senses. From it, the phantasm is derived. Then, from the phantasm, the agent intellect draws out what can be known, i.e., the intelligible species.

Without the element of the sensible, *intellectus* cannot function. The body, therefore, is essential to *intellectus* because the body is necessary for the actualization of the potentiality of the *intellectus*. *Intellectus* is not actualized without the body.[57] But body is necessarily characterized by gender and, hence, knowing is formed and affected by gender.

Returning to our example of Mary at the Annunciation, we see that her ability to recognize something greater than herself, her ability to conform to it, and her ability to carry it within herself, as a part of herself, all serve as an illustration of the way in which the human *intellectus* actively receives and ultimately knows.

At the same time, within *Fides et Ratio*, we find three main guidelines for rectifying philosophy. Underlying these we can decipher a unique feminine element. The pope writes that philosophy must first recover its "sapiential dimension." This dimension is the capacity to recognize a meaning that is greater than the human knower and to conform to that greater being rather than be trapped within its own narrow confines.[58]

Secondly, philosophy must "verify the human capacity to *know the truth*, to come to a knowledge which can reach objective truth by means of that *adaequatio rei et intellectus* to which the Scholastic Doctors referred."[59]

Thirdly, philosophy must have a metaphysical range; it must be capable of "transcending empirical data in order to attain something absolute."[60]

III.

Some might think it a stretch to have gone this far in emphasizing the feminine element of knowing, but recall that the relationship between the Church and God is that of bride and groom. That relationship is defined by the Revelation of God and the Church's acceptance of it, which is no more and no less, the work of philosophy and theology and the work of each one of us. Christ the bridegroom has given himself. His bride accepts the gift of her spouse and responds with the gift of herself. In his *Mulieris Dignitatem*, the Pope explains that this symbol of the bride applies to all men and women by virtue of the spousal relationship between Christ and the Church: "In this way 'being the bride,' and thus the 'feminine' element, becomes the symbol of all that is 'human,' according to the words of Paul: 'There is neither male nor female; for you are *all one* in Christ Jesus' (Gal. 3,28)."[61]

This, however, does not create tension between men and women, or between the masculine and feminine characteristics. From the beginning, God intended that man and woman should exist together. The battle between the sexes, so to speak, exists because of original sin, not because of the differences themselves. In their creation, God intended them to share a life together, one ordered towards knowing him. It makes sense, therefore, that they would complement each other in the intellectual life, in the way they come to know. To respond, however, to the love of the groom, as the Church must do, is a feminine response. Mary exemplifies this response and hence is the paradigm of the human vocation, particularly the human vocation to be both philosopher[62] and bride.

The intellect and the will enable the human person to be truly free. Therefore, the intellect must be fully developed, both in its active and receptive qualities. Man and woman have been given a life to share together. Generally speaking, we can see where they each exemplify different qualities or abilities. Using the thought of Aquinas as a springboard, we can better understand the complementarity that should exist in the intellectual life of each person, regardless of how many degrees he or she may possess. We are witnessing what happens as we leave aside the feminine, actively receptive side of knowing and culture. I think the case can also be made that we are seeing what happens when the masculine is not complemented by the feminine, and we are beginning to see a culture and frame of thought that is devoid not only of the feminine, but also of the masculine.

The pope calls philosophy the mirror which reflects the culture of people.[63] Later, in *Novo Millenio Inuente*, he recalls the anthropological and vocational character of the Church which parallels this understanding of philosophy:

> A new century, a new millennium are opening in the light of Christ. But not everyone can see this light. Ours is the wonderful and demanding task of becoming its 'reflection.' This is the *mysterium lunae*, which was much a part of the contemplation of the Fathers of the Church, who employed this image to show the Church's dependence on Christ, the Sun whose light she reflects. It was a way of expressing what Christ himself said when he called himself the 'light' of the world' (Jn 8:12) and asked his disciples to be 'the light of the world' (Mt 5:14). This is a daunting task if we consider our human weakness, which so often renders us

opaque and full of shadows. But it is a task which we can
accomplish if we turn to the light of Christ and open ourselves to the grace which makes us a new creation.[64]

Indeed, the future of the Church depends upon recapturing the
element of the feminine, particularly as exemplified by Mary, who is
also the paradigm of philosophers. But we must always keep in mind
that the feminine and masculine are never known independently of
one another. It also depends upon our notions of masculinity if we
are to restore the sense of the feminine, and if we are to take the
Church forward into the new millennium.

Pia Francesca de Solenni is the first American winner of the Prize
of the Pontifical Academies in Rome. A 1993 graduate of Thomas
Aquinas College in Santa Paula, California, she received the "distinguished" mark for the defense of her doctoral thesis at the University
of the Holy Cross in Rome. Her thesis was an analysis of feminist
theories in the light of the philosophy of St. Thomas Aquinas. Her
work underlines the equality of men and women, emphasizes the fact
that both are made in the image and likeness of God, and stresses that
the basic vocation of both has a strong intellectual component, that
of knowing God. The thesis was, and her work continues to be,
deemed outstanding for its original scientific and cultural contributions, rooted in Christian thought.

Notes

1   Pseudo-Ephiphanius, Homily in Praise of Holy Mary Mother of God:
    PG 43, 493.
2   *Fides et Ratio*, John Paul II, 1998, n. 108.
3   *Fides*, n. 57; *Aeterni Patris*, Leo XII, 1879, n. 109
4   *Fides*, n. 61.
5   *Fides*, n. 7.
6   *Fides*, n. 10–11; Cf. n. 34: "He [Jesus] is the *eternal Word* in whom all
    things were created, and he is the *incarnate Word* who in his entire per-
    son [cf. *Dei Verbum*, n. 4] reveals the Father (cf. *Jn* 1:14, 18)."
7   *Letter to Women*, John Paul II, 1995, n. 11.
8   *Letter*, n. 11; Cf. *Evangelium Vitae*, John Paul II, 1995, n. 99.
9   Cf. Wisdom 6,12–20; 7,7–8.
10 Cf. Sirach 14,20–27.
11 *Fides*, n. 18.

12 Cf. Luke 1,5–55.

13 *Fides*, n.28 & 33.

14 *Fides*, n. 17.

15 Cf. *De Veritate* 2.2; *Summa Theologiae I*, q. 32, a.2, c.

16 *Fides*, n. 31.

17 Cf. Stern, Karl, *The Flight from Woman*, Farrar, Straus, and Giroux, New York, 1965.

18 ST *I*, q.93, a.6, ad 2.

19 ST *I*, q.76, a.1, c.; NB: Aquinas says here that the soul *is* the form of the body, not that it *forms* the body.

20 Archideo, Lila Blanca, "Bases para una antropología femenina," *Atti del IX Congresso Tomistico Internazionale*, Libreria Editrice Vaticana, Vatican City 1991, p.102: "La cogitativa entonces al ser una potencia que distingue a una persona de otra por su acción intelectual y volitiva, es decir por los específico de la naturaleza human y al constituirse en puente entre la sensibilidad y el entendimiento en el conocer y actuar humanos, tiene que ver fundamentalmente con el orden en la estructura psico-ética de la persona ya que señala sus funciones propiamente humanas."

21 Cf. Steenberghen, Ferdnand Van, *Epistemology*, Joseph F. Wagner Inc., New York 1949, p. 61; Cf. ST *I*, q.12, a.4, c. In this text, Aquinas specifically addresses whether created intellect can know the divine essence through natural things. What we know, we know according to our *mode* of knowing. For man and woman, this means a knowing that necessarily involves bodily senses.

22 ST *I*, q.79, a.8, sc.

23 ST *I*, q.93, a.6 c. Prior to this in *I*, q.93, a.4, c., Aquinas speaks of both man's rational nature and his intellectual nature, signifying the same thing.

24 *SCG*, IV.11.

25 ST *I*, q.79, a.1, c.

26 Cf. ST *I*, q.93, a.7, ad 2.

27 *Super I Cor.* XV, 1, 11; Also cited in part by MacIntyre in *Dependent Rational Animals*, Duckworth, London 1999, p. 6.

28 Note that when speaking of the perfection of the intellect here, the perfection is not one of mere scientific knowledge. Rather, the intellect is the seat of the soul's ability to see and know God. This point will be further developed in this paper.

29 ST *I*, q.79, a.2, c.

30 ST *I*, q.79, a.2, c.

31 ST *I*, q.79, a.2, c.

32 Aristotle, *De Anima*, 429b29.

33 Cf. Aquinas, *De Libris De Anima*, III, ix.722.

34 Aristotle, *De Anima*, 429a10–25; Cf. ST *I-II*, q.22, a.1 c.: *"Nam secundum receptionem tantum, dicitur quod sentire et intelligere est quoddam pati."*

35 Gilson, Etienne, *The Christian Philosophy of St. Thomas Aquinas*, translated by L. K. Shook, University of Notre Dame Press, Indiana 1994, p. 207.

36 ST *I*, q.79, a.3, c.

37 Cf. Gilson, Etienne, *Christian Philosophy in the Middle Ages*, Sheed and Ward, London 1955, p. 377: "It is the perfection of the agent intellect to contain them virtually and to be capable of forming them, but it is also its weakness to be able to form them only in connection with our perception of sensible things. The origin of human knowledge is therefore in the senses."

38 ST *I*, q.54, a.4, c.

39 ST *I*, q.84, a.7, ad 2; Cf. ST *I*, q.85, a.1, ad 3: *"Sed phantasmata, cum sint similitudines individuorum, et existant in organis corporeis."*

40 Cf. Gilson, Etienne, *The Christian Philosophy of St. Thomas Aquinas*, p. 218: "The proper object of the human intellect is quiddity; that is, nature existing in a particular corporeal matter. Thus it is in ours to know the idea of stone, but the nature of such and such a determined stone. This nature is the result of the union between a form and its proper matter. Similarly, the abstract concept "horse" is not presented to our mind as an object. It is the nature, rather, of a horse that has been realized in a given, determined, concrete horse. In other words, it is easy to discern in the objects of human knowledge a universal and intelligible element which is associated with a particular and material element. The proper operation of the agent intellect is to dissociate these two elements in order to furnish the possible intellect with the intelligible and universal which lay implied in the sensible."

41 ST *I*, q.78, a.1, c.

42 Cf. ST *I-II*, q.94, a.2 c.

43 ST *I*, q.79, a.7, c.: *"Unde patet quod memoria non est alia potentia ab intellectu: ad rationem enim potentiae passivae pertinet conservare, sicut et recipere."*

44 ST *I*, q.79, a.8, c.

45 ST *I*, q.79, a.8, c. Cf. *De Veritate*, q.15, a.1, c. Here Aquinas also examines this relationship of *intellectus* to *ratio*. In the context of the question of whether the *intellectus* and *ratio* are diverse potencies in the human person, he lists many of their individual characteristics and goes on to show that they are still the same faculty. These individual characteristics are key for understanding the differences between the two aspects. *Ratio*

judges, *intellectus* comprehends. They are acts which are compared to motion and rest. However, the principle of rest and motion is the same. When the mind knows truth perfectly, it is in virtue of *intellectus*. When the truth is not immediately known, there is need of discourse, discussion or what Aquinas calls *discursus*.

46 *De Anima*, III, 1.11. n. 751.

47 *Summa Contra Gentiles*, IV.11, 3477. The word *studio* here has the sense of diligence or work, a labor to be accomplished.

48 ST *I*, q.78, a.4.

49 ST *I*, q.78, a.4, c.

50 ST *I*, q.93, a.4, ad. 1.; *Supplementum*, q. 39, a.1.; IV *Sententiarum*, dist. 25, q. 2, a. 1.; ST *I*, q.93, a.6, ad 2.

51 Cf. ST *I*, q.76, a.2, c; Cf. Kenny, Anthony, *Aquinas on Mind*, Routledge, New York 1993, p. 152–53.

52 Cf. Traina, Cristina L. H., *Feminist Ethics and Natural Law: The End of the Anathemas*, Georgetown University Press, Washington, D.C. 1999, p. 65: "Memory's residence in the sensitive part of the soul ties experiential knowledge securely to the body."

53 Cf. Dancy, Jonathan and Sosa, Ernest, Editors, *A Companion to Epistemology*, Blackwell 1992, p. 20.

54 Cf. Rábade Romeo, Sergio, *Estructura del conocer humano*, Gregoria del Toro, Madrid 1966, pp. 56–57.

55 ST *I*, q.79, a.8, c.

56 Gilson, *The Christian Philosophy of St. Thomas Aquinas*, p. 211.

57 ST I, q.87, a.1, c.

58 *Fides*, n. 81.

59 *Fides*, n. 82.

60 *Fides*, n. 83.

61 *Mulieris Dignitatem*, John Paul II, 1988, n. 25.

62 *Fides*, n. 64.

63 *Fides*, n. 103.

64 *Novo*, n. 58.

THOUGHTS ON PIA DE SOLENNI'S "FIDES ET RATIO: A CONTEXT FOR DEVELOPING THE NEW FEMINISM"
Elizabeth Fox-Genovese

In the paper you have just heard, Dr. Solenni offers us a fresh contribution to the growing discussion about the possibilities for a "new feminism" – a feminism compatible with the basic tenets of Catholicism, faithful to the Magisterium, and withal respectful of women. Few would contest the crying need for such a new feminism or deny that Pope John Paul II has broken new ground in exhorting Catholics to contribute to the formulation and living of it. He has consistently encouraged Catholic women to reflect upon their condition and vocation, just as he has criticized not merely those feminists who seek to abolish all differences between women and men, but those religious conservatives who seek to perpetuate women's subordination to and dependence upon men.

The Holy Father's Letter to Women of 1995 expresses his conviction that there can be no "honest and permanent" solutions to the issues and problems that affect women if they are not "based on the recognition of the inherent, inalienable dignity of women, and the importance of women's presence and participation in all aspects of social life" (38). For recognition "of the dignity of every human being," he insists, "is the foundation and support of the concept of universal human rights" (38).

Predictably, secular feminists have had no patience with the Holy Father's position, which they typically dismiss with ill-disguised scorn, reserving their special wrath for his claims that "woman's singular relationship with human life derives from her vocation to motherhood," that "the maternal mission is also the basis of a particular responsibility," and that "the woman is called to offer the best of herself to the baby growing within her," since "it is precisely by making herself 'gift' that she comes to know herself better and is fulfilled in her femininity"(26). Most openly deplore the pope's insistence that women's employment must always respect the "fundamental duty" of the "most delicate tasks of motherhood" (27), rejecting the suggestion that women's rights include any binding duties at all.

Doctor de Solenni applauds the Holy Father's defense of women; but, by means of a clever and thought-provoking gambit, she essentially bypasses the specific issues he discusses. Turning away from the heated debates about women's position in the world and in the Church, she focuses upon a passage in his encyclical *Fides et Ratio* and then turns to its roots in Aquinas to argue for the longstanding theological recognition of the intellectual equality of women and men. In the measure that she discusses motherhood at all, she does so in relation to the Virgin Mary – not in relation to the lives of contemporary women. Thus does she move the conversation from the level of everyday life, legal systems, and public policy to the level of what secular feminists reverently evoke as "theory."

Sharing Dr. Solenni's admiration for the Angelic Doctor, I have nothing but sympathy and respect for her argument. And which of us cannot but delight in seeing the feminist debates elevated to the rarified atmosphere of serious philosophy and theology? My questions about her paper do not so much concern what we might call her "philosophical turn," as they concern the cogency of her arguments and, especially, the ways in which she expects them to contribute to the new feminism we are all seeking.

Dr. de. Solenni, invoking Aquinas, simultaneously insists upon the equality of women and men's minds and the significance of their physiological – or embodied – differences. Thus, she attributes great importance to the distinction between feminine and masculine modes of thought, but never really defines either feminine or masculine. Her reading of Aquinas seems intended to support the common understanding of feminine as passive and masculine as active, yet she properly insists than men, every bit as much as women, participate in the feminine "passivity" of the Church as the bride of Christ. Without pretending to do justice to the details of her discussion of Aquinas, I should like to suggest that the possibility for the coexistence of equality and difference constitutes the main theoretical and practical challenge to and problem for feminism, whether old or new, secular or faith-based.

My principal criticism of Dr. de Solenni's argument, as presented here, concerns her seeming reluctance even to acknowledge the existence of the problem. At one point, in passing, she refers to the equality of souls and of intellects and then invokes St. Paul's frequently quoted passage from Galatians 3:28: "There is neither Jew nor Greek, there is neither slave nor free, there is neither male nor female; for you are all one in Christ Jesus." However we may seek to interpret that passage today, we cannot escape the hard truth that, throughout most of the history of Christianity, Christians understood the passage to be entirely compatible with slavery, serfdom, and the subordination of women, among innumerable other forms of social hierarchy. Christians may have been enjoined to recognize themselves as all part of one body, but they also knew that any body has a head and feet and they differ in function and prerogatives. Intrinsic worth and equality in the eye of God were not commonly taken to dictate equality in this world, and the radicals who did so take them were usually condemned as heretics.

Aquinas took the hierarchical structure of his world for granted, as did the vast majority of Europeans – and non-Europeans – until the great revolutions of the seventeenth and eighteenth centuries proclaimed and began to implement the principles of individualism and equality. Full implementation proved a protracted undertaking. The question of women's equality with men arose at the outset, but did not gain widespread adherence until the final third of the twentieth century. The period between the enunciation of the principle of equality and its implementation nonetheless revealed the formidable difficulty of reconciling equality with difference within prevailing individualist premises. The logic of equality and individualism has carried feminism to its daunting string of victories, which seem to be culminating in a public denial of the legitimacy of physiological differences between women and men.

It is difficult – if not impossible – to dodge the conclusion that "equal but different" has not played well in modern and postmodern individualist societies. The moral force of equality has increasingly swept all but economic divisions – which it increasingly appears to serve – before it. Under these conditions, the restoration of a morally acceptable vision of equal but different stands as the foremost challenge of our times – and not merely to feminism. Meeting that challenge will almost certainly require the restoration of an idea of legitimate authority – natural and divine – which alone can justify the attribution of different functions, responsibilities, and prerogatives to different groups. I am hard pressed to imagine a more daunting challenge or a more pressing need, and I am sure that however important our intellectual work, we cannot rise to the occasion through theory alone.

In this perspective, I regret that Dr. de Solenni did not, however briefly, touch upon some of the most compelling contemporary issues that any new feminism must confront. Like it or not, the destinies and vocations of women remain central to the future of our world. In this, the Holy Father is right: women must remain the bearers and nurturers of the culture of life, independent of whether any specific woman bears a child. There are no easy answers to the question of how we defend women's equality to men in dignity and respect as members of Christ's body and in the world while also defending their difference from men. But if we fail passionately and insistently to seek solutions in practice, we will fail to defend a culture of life, which is to say that we cannot fruitfully discuss women's equality to and difference from men without considering the relation of our theory to the realities of legalized abortion and all that lies beyond it.

Elizabeth Fox-Genovese is currently the Eleonore Raoul Professor of the Humanities at Emory University in Atlanta. She received her A.B. degree from Bryn Mawr College (1963); and her M.A. (1966) and Ph.D.(1974) from Harvard University. Among her areas of interest and specialization are comparative women's history; the antebellum South; and cultural, literary, and intellectual history.

Among her most recent publications are Feminism without Illusions: A Critique of Individualism (1991); "Feminism Is Not the Story of my Life": How Today's Feminist Elite Has Lost Touch with the Real Concerns of Women (1996); Reconstructing History: The Emergence of a Historical Society, co-edited with Elisabeth Lasch-Quinn (1999); and Women and the Future of the Family, with responses by Stanley J. Grenz, Mardi Keyes, Mary Stewart Van Leeuwen, Ed., James W. Skillen & Michelle N. Voll (2000).

FOR BETTER OR FOR WORSE: CATHOLICS AND THE MEDIA
Kathryn Jean Lopez

Thank you so much for having me here. It is a terribly clichéd beginning for a speech, but in this case it is the honest truth: It is an honor for me to be here. Catholic education has long been a top priority in my life. I was born to two Catholic elementary-school teachers, each of whom would become Catholic elementary-school principals while I was still myself in (yet another) Catholic elementary school – we were a multi-school family!

It was always a source of pride for my father that he entered Catholic education in the first grade and never left it. And with his every day he showed why that was something to be proud of, as my mother continues to do today.

So I know how important the work you do is, literally following in Christ's ministerial footsteps, teaching as He did. And I know many of the complications – mostly because I grew up with Catholic education at the dinner table, on summer vacations, and everywhere else; and partly because I got caught up in some Catholic-identity issues while I was at the Catholic University of America (I mean the *school* had the identity issues, not me – just wanted to clarify!). While I was there – much less than a decade ago – it was not the proudly *Catholic* Catholic University that it is today under the wonderful Fr. O'Connell.

I say all this by way of letting you know that you have my utmost admiration.

Now that I have, hopefully, flattered you enough, please bear with me because the groups I most often speak to are: 1) high school and college students; and 2) TV and radio-talk-show audiences. So, be kind.

Now, I am certain that speech-writing books probably warn that a speaker should *never* start off with a plea to the audience avoid laughing, but given what I am about to say, my plea may be called for. So, please don't laugh (or get too mad) about what I am about to say. Here goes: We Catholics have a lot to thank the media for.

Bill Donohue from the Catholic League isn't here, is he? I'm not sure I would want him to hear me say that. Seriously, though, I think Bill Donohue would probably agree with me to some extent. In George Weigel's new book, *The Courage to be Catholic* – which is, by the way, hands down, the best book to have been written in the wake of the "scandals" that have been in the news since the start of the year (Michael Novak says: buy a dozen copies and pass them out to priests, family members, friends, and reporters) – anyway, in this book, Weigel writes: "If God could work through the Assyrians in the Old Testament, God can certainly work through the *New York Times* and the *Boston Globe* today, whether the *Times* or the *Globe* realize what's happening or not."

I am going to continue to steal from Weigel. He writes: "The Church owes the press a debt of gratitude. Because of the press, some sexual predators have been arrested and jailed. Because of the press, the authorities were able to locate predators like Paul Shanley and former Dallas priest Rudy Kos before they could do any more damage to young minds and souls; in both instances, Church leaders had failed to protect either the Church or society. Because of the press, the Catholic Church has been forced to recognize that it is in more trouble than its leaders and lay people might have imagined."

He is absolutely right. That is not to say, however, that the *Boston Globe* – which has been the source for so much of the scandal news – has not been anti-Catholic in the past, present, or future. That is not to say that Connie Chung has any clue what she is talking about when she parks herself in front of St. Peter's in Rome to report on the American cardinals meeting with the pope, as she did last spring. She doesn't. No clue. Nor is she helping anyone when she brings on dissenters and asks them why the Catholic Church has this abuse problem everyone is talking about. Because the Catholic Church oppresses women, of course: that is among the answers a dissenting sister gives Connie – among other wrong answers. And so to express a little gratitude for the media doing their job does not mean that I am saying that the mainstream media generally provided much sane, rational context to the hyper-blitz of coverage which they provided in the starting months of this year. They, of course, did not provide *any* context!

This is why the media needs you – the people in this room. But more on that later.

It follows that to express some gratitude to the press does not mean that the secular press "gets" the scandals, or the root of the problems, or what allowed them to happen; those roots lie in the culture of dissent that has been so much a part of Catholic culture in the United States since Vatican II. For most of the media world – with the exception of some conservative publications like my own *National Review* – the word "homosexuality" is never uttered in reference to the scandals. About the only time it was brought up in polite society was the day ·Joaquin Navarro-Valls, the Vatican spokesman, raised the possibility that homosexuals should not be admitted to the seminaries, setting off the firestorm of an anti-straight, male-patriarchy backlash. (Never expect rational, informed debate.)

So what should Catholics think about the media? And how should Catholics engage the media? In keeping with the theme of this conference, "Voices of the New Springtime," I submit to you the name of another book, this one recently released by Loyola Press. It was written by a young reporter named Colleen Carroll; it is called *The New Faithful: Why Young Adults Are Embracing Christian Orthodoxy*. It is not specifically Catholic, this book, but it has a lot of Catholic stuff in it (and Carroll is, herself, Catholic). But the book is about young orthodox Christians who are active in their respective churches, and who are idealistic, enthusiastic, public witnesses to their faith. The book is a terrific antidote (as World Youth Day was in Canada this summer) to the depressing spectacle of the many dissenting Catholic voices which the media always manages to find to put on the air or quote. It is a refreshing alternative to the public face of Catholics as this has been so often portrayed by the media – See: It didn't take long for me to turn on the media!

I think that we Catholics need to do a better job with the media by taking a page out of Frances Kissling's playbook. Of course, Kissling is a somewhat unique case. She is president of something called Catholics for a Free Choice. It is most appropriate to put the word "Catholics" in their title in quotation marks, of course. Catholics for a Free Choice is essentially one media-savvy woman, a small staff, a website, and a fax machine – and lots of abortion-industry money – lobbying the media. She is really just being used by the abortion industry to make sure that abortion is never rare.

Forget that "safe, legal, and rare" stuff, by the way – few committed abortion advocates ever wanted that. Indeed, Kissling herself once even ran an abortion clinic. Still, she manages to sell herself to the media as the legitimate counter to the official word of the "patriarchal" Catholic Church (this despite the fact that she has zero membership base).

Academics who actually agree with what the Church teaches – who are smart, happy, and well-adjusted people, like many of you in this room – should be on the silly talking-heads shows, and should show up more on the op-ed pages of something other than our own, safe, preaching-to-the-choir publications – certainly more than a Frances Kissling does.

Don't get me wrong: as a primary editor of a leading conservative online magazine and print magazine, and a writer for many various other publications – none of which includes the *New York Times!* – I do see the tremendous value in those preaching-to-the-choir venues that many of us write for. They are giving the choir the ammunition, the facts, that the choir needs to be armed with. If they are cool enough – which, on many days, *National Review Online* is, I say it in all modesty! – they will even penetrate into the mainstream. Besides, the choir is not always unanimous, anyway.

So, besides writing for your Catholic university's law review – which you should – and for *NR* and *Crisis* and *The National Catholic Register, Catholic World Report, Our Sunday Visitor,* and the like – you should also try to write for the papers more people read with their coffee in the morning.

For instance, Anne Hendershott, a smart gal professor at the University of San Diego (who, by the way, has a new book out, well worth reading, called *The Politics of Deviance*) recently sent me a great little piece on the recent General Electric sonogram commercials. They really are remarkable commercials. I sat on her piece, as I sometimes tend to do, and so she asked me if she could take it from me and submit it elsewhere. Well, thank God for my procrastination, because it meant that it got published in the Sunday edition of the *San Diego Tribune.* Many more readers of the *San Diego Tribune* needed to hear a happy, positive, pro-life message than my readers – and from a Catholic woman. I would love to survey the media to find out how many reporters and editors think all pro-lifers are male!

So, in other words, what the media needs from us is constant education – precisely what all of you do best! The media also need engagement from us (no matter how futile it may seem most of the time).

And the same approach goes way beyond sonogram commercials. In many ways, and on many of the most important issues of the day – literally life and death issues – the Catholic Church is "the Teacher." Short of a Leon Kass, who is not exactly in every American home, I do not know many people who can explain the evils and the facts about abortion and cloning better than a Robert George. The newspaper and TV coverage of these issues tend to be absolutely – completely – useless. Just this week, I watched Katie Couric on *The Today Show* interview Christopher Reeve in his home about his amazing progress since his paralyzing accident. America's Sweetheart set Superman up to provide viewers with a lecture on how his progress had been made possible though arduous effort, despite pro-life efforts to stop life-saving research. Most Americans today get their bioethics news from Christopher Reeve and Michael J. Fox on the Larry King Show. Simply put, in that narrow media world, the folks in this room are considered anti-Superman, anti-Alex P. Keaton. We are unconcerned about someone's father dying because we would rather preserve a blob of cells.

How's that for the odds being stacked against you and your argument? And against the truth? Who's going to argue when that is the case? The odds really are stacked against us in many ways when it comes to the "Brave New World" issues. It is not even called cloning by most of the media and by many politicians, and certainly not by the biotech folks. Rather, it is "somatic-cell nuclear transplantation"! And even when it is admitted to be cloning, there is a false distinction made between what is being called "therapeutic cloning," and what is styled "research cloning." The president's Bioethics Commission, which some members of the Fellowship of Catholic Scholars are a crucial part of, did an important job in trying to define the terms and get back to the basic facts. If you have not yet read their report, you really should. It is accessible on-line and will be hitting bookstores in a few weeks. (I am sorry, by the way, that I keep recommending books. I'm sure you have had enough of that this weekend already!)

We really are at a turning point on many of these issues, as some of the other speakers have addressed more thoroughly than I can do. Upon presenting the Bioethics Commission's cloning report to President Bush, Leon Kass, the head of the Commission, wrote in the report's Introduction: "Human cloning, we are confident, is but a foretaste – the herald of many dazzling genetic and reproductive technologies that will raise profound moral questions well into the future."

It is important to get this one right, because it will haunt all future decisions. We have done test-tube babies; we have opened egg and sperm banks; we see ads in college newspapers offering cash-strapped college girls thousands of dollars for their eggs. Just this week, in fact, someone sent me a recent issue of Columbia University's campus paper; in it was an ad offering $10,000 for a young woman's eggs. Even so, cloning is a whole new ballgame from which human dignity may not be able to recover.

Still, it is not yet altogether too late to stop. As Leon Kass has written: "[O]ur technologies of bio-psycho-engineering are still in their infancy, and in some ways they make all too clear what they might look like in their full maturity." These kinds of problems are *our* issues, and there is no reason why we should let the culture of life lose.

You do yeomen's work in the higher education. But Catholics simply need to use the media more, as the Left does so well and so often.

Back to cloning for a second: This session of Congress will soon end, and there will have been absolutely no progress on the issue of cloning. No ban, no moratorium. No ban even on the bogus distinction. That is quite remarkable when you think about it. It is really incredible, too, when you remember that but a few weeks before September 11, 2001, when embryonic-stem-cell research was all over the news, Tom Daschle vowed: "I am opposed to the effort to clone under virtually any circumstances that I can think of."

By the way, you do not want me to get started on the issue of stem cells, an issue where accurate reporting may, in fact, be impossible, given the media track record. All this points to the fact that the media needs us. It needs you. It needs *teachers*.

On a recent *Talkback Live* appearance – if you have been on it or seen it, you know this is among the most painful shows on television, and you also know that I am not trying to impress you by telling you that I have been on this program – because the words "I was on Talkback Live" could be the most humiliating in our language. Anyway, on this debate show, I was put up against another conservative chick who had recently been wined and dined by top Saudi officials. Our segment had been preceded by one with Saudi Arabia's top spin-doctor in the U.S. The other woman, a talk-radio host, got more face-time from the host because she has actually been to Saudi Arabia – if even only as part of a propaganda junket – so while my few sound bites about the lack of freedom there (including religious freedom) were not exactly verbose, at least the audience, between actual paid-for commercials about Saudi Arabia, got a taste of another point of view.

That is what it will often be like, as some of you already know. But when you get e-mails and phone calls, get stopped at the supermarket by people whom you made an impression on, then you will realize that it is not all for naught. And, more so, I think, this is true with those producers, hosts, and bookers, who, with every articulate defender of the faith they see – they help them make good television, after all – will begin to realize that the Catholic Church may be something more than their stereotype of it.

In this vein, I think that it is vitally important for us to help train young people to be articulate voices in defense of the Church. That's why I have gotten involved with the Cardinal Newman Society for the Preservation of Catholic Higher Education. At schools where the voices of authentic Catholicism – versus dissent and or secular elitism – are muted, it is important to support students who want to have a non-dissenting outlet on campus: a happy, well-adjusted, Catholic voice. You would hope that this would be the main campus newspaper, or a view promoted by the administration. Unfortunately, however, as many of you know all too well and first-hand, that is not always the case. Unfortunately too, not all colleges and universities are run by the likes of Father O'Connell, who saved my alma mater from the fate it was preparing for itself while I was there under another president (and his string of predecessors).

But I don't need to tell this audience all that. Besides the witness you provide in the classroom, at the schools where you are, you might also be an important support for those students who want to help the campus to be truly Catholic, in the spirit of *Ex Corde Ecclesiae*. Feel free to give them my e-mail address: it is klopez@nationalreview.com. I will be happy to introduce them to fellow travelers at Boston College, Holy Cross, Georgetown, and other schools that have authentically Catholic voices in the form of alternative campus papers. To help provide a support system for those kids who have papers, or who want to start papers, the Cardinal Newman Society has started a Catholic Campus Media Network.

One of the most important lessons all of us must learn from the horrible scandals that have plagued the headlines since the start of this year is that the culture of dissent has failed, and that we truly are now at the beginning of a New Springtime. Groups like Voice of the Faithful that have been popping up to claim to be the new voice of Catholicism are, for the most part, simply dissenters who think they have the answer to many of the problems that their views, in fact, helped cause.

The media need to know that we are out there, that we are university administrators, professors, recent graduates, and media voices even – and that we are not hiding our heads, we are not ashamed to be Catholic. In fact, we even like the Catholic Church, and we know what it is about, and we try to do our part to spread the Gospel the Church is based on through our daily lives and work.

If any of you out there have a Mr. Moneybags, get an effort funded as the Left so often manages to do – an effort to inundate the media with your – our – presence. Until then, I encourage you to do your part, as I know so many of you are already doing, to be leaders, and to mold new young leaders in to be at the public forefront of this New Springtime. Of course, it is the example of your leadership that will do so much of that molding. You inspire your students, your colleagues, your children.

If you are so inclined, though, educate through the bullhorn of the media as well. Whether it be by op-eds, feeding a reporter information, or by silly TV debate-show appearances, the effort is worthwhile. The media are rarely allies. When they turn out to be allies, as often as not it is unintentional – as in the case of the clerical sex abuse scandals this year. But still, I think, rather than accusing them of anti-Catholicism, or calling them on the various examples of their hostility toward religion and faithful people – however true it might be, and believe me, I understand it is true; Ken Woodward, for example, in the current *First Things*, calls anti-Catholicism "the last acceptable prejudice" – we should still do our part to engage them as much as possible. And a key to that is to educate them through that engagement.

Thanks again for having me here, for listening to me, and for bearing with me. And, before I forget, feel free to get in contact with me – among other things I am always looking for ideas and to be educated myself as part of my duties as the gal who decides what goes up on *National Review Online* every morning. (By the way, the address for NRO is www.nationalreview.com. If you haven't discovered it yet, but are interested in such things, it is a daily publication published in addition to our more traditional print magazine, *National Review*. If you want it, my e-mail address, as mentioned above is klopez@nationalreview.com. Reporters and editors are only as good as their contacts, and this happens to be a top-notch source for contacts, so do please feel free to "holler."

Kathryn Jean Lopez is an Associate Editor at *National Review* and the Executive Editor of *National Review Online*. She is a graduate of the Catholic University of America in Washington, D.C., where she studied political theory and philosophy. Before joining *National Review*, she worked at the Heritage Foundation, a conservative think tank on Capitol Hill. Her writing has appeared in *The Washington Times, Heterodoxy, The Woman's Quarterly, The National Catholic Register, Human Events, American Outlook, New York Press,* and *The Human Life Review*, among other publications. She is a frequent guest on radio and TV shows, and has appeared on CNN, Fox News Channel, MSNBC, and "Oxygen," as well as internationally.

DEMOCRACY, SECULARISM, AND RELIGIOUS FAITH IN AMERICA
Robert P. George

I.

As American citizens, we participate in an experiment in ordered liberty and a regime of democratic republican government. Not all Americans are religious believers – people of faith – but most of us are. A much higher percentage of Americans than, say, French, or Italians, or English, believe in God, attend weekly worship services, and pray regularly. And this is no recent phenomenon. Tocqueville noted the remarkable religiosity of Americans more than a hundred-and-fifty years ago. Although faith was perceived as the enemy of freedom in late-eighteenth and early nineteenth century Europe, it seemed even then to be integrally bound up with the American conception of freedom. Indeed, the American conception of freedom seems to have been shaped by the religious faith of Americans.

But surely it has worked the other way round, too. So I invite you to reflect with me on the question of the impact of our particular form of civic order – as it has actually developed – on the religious practice and faith of Americans. In particular, what has been the impact of our civic order on the American conception of the free exercise of religion?

The matter immediately poses a methodological challenge. Strictly speaking, there is no "faith of Americans." There are, rather, "faiths" – plural. And it is to be expected that the interaction of faith and American democracy will vary significantly depending on the nature of the particular faith in question. Even *within* broad communities of faith (such as Catholicism, Protestantism, and Judaism) democracy's impact upon religion – and its free exercise – has been different for different individuals and subcommunities.

The experience of Orthodox Jews has differed from the experience of Reform Jews; the experience of mainline Protestants has differed from that of Evangelicals. Getting hold of any *one* of these experiences requires a grasp of the religious convictions, of the structure of communal life, and of what may be called the spirituality that, all together, largely *constitute* the faith and the community of faith; and beyond that, of course, knowledge in history, sociology, and perhaps other disciplines is required. I am tempted to plead that I lack the time in this lecture to do the subject justice; the true culprit, however, is my lack of learning.

I am at best an amateur theologian, and, as my colleagues in sociology and history at Princeton would enthusiastically assure you, I am no sociologist or historian at all. But I have some sense of the course of our particular faith – Catholicism – through American history. That history sheds a certain light upon our topic; for Catholicism has been suspected and derided, in season and out, as a peculiarly *undemocratic* religion, more than faintly *un-American*.

Please be assured that I pause over this perennial suspicion and criticism not to settle accounts or to call for reparations. I pause because we can learn from it the articulated *expectations* that the American regime has of religion. Unless we naively suppose the regime to have been wholly ineffectual in shaping belief to its needs, we can infer from these expectations (or demands) something of a global answer to our question, elements of a comprehensive account. Here we have a common hydraulic pressure, a centripetal force ranging across the various faiths, impelling them to a common center. Call it an answer from the top down, truly faith *under* democracy. Of course, we can leave it to the specialists – the historians and sociologists of religion – to gauge the precise extent to which a particular religion has been shaped by this force.

The Bill of Particulars in the indictment against Catholicism has been remarkably constant. But one charge was effaced by the course of *European* history: the claim that Catholics owed allegiance to a foreign *temporal* prince. That charge was characteristically joined to one that survives: Catholicism is undemocratic because it compromises the individual's proper spiritual autonomy. Related to *this* accusation is another charge: that *politically* Catholics do not think for themselves. They instead follow slavishly the dictates of their priests, where they do not serve contemptible party bosses, or both. Catholics have long been said to behave undemocratically by not trusting their personal religious "experience" as a guide to authentic spiritual life; rather, they hold to "immutable" (read: ossified) "metaphysical" truths. Between World War II and the Second Vatican Council, Catholics were criticized for rejecting the linchpin of democracy, the First Amendment's "separation of church and state."

Finally, perhaps the central charge made *since* Vatican II: Catholics behave undemocratically by trying to "impose their morality" upon others in defiance of the principles of our pluralistic democracy, especially regarding abortion, and now embryo experimentation and matters of sexual morality as well. This charge could only have arisen, as it did, after the abandonment by so many other churches and communities of faith of the common Judaeo-Christian morality, or of a commitment to a decent public morality, or both.

No wonder politically ambitious Catholics from William J. Brennan (in his Senate confirmation hearings) to John F. Kennedy to Mario Cuomo felt obliged to say that they would separate their religion from their public responsibilities. To my knowledge, members of no other church were similarly expected to privatize their faith and give public attestation to their doing so. In many cases, perhaps, it was taken for granted, because of the nature of their faith, that they already had.

II.

The abiding commitment of our cultural, political, and legal authorities to a specifically "democratic" religion explains more – much more, in my judgment – about our constitutional law of church and state than anything Madison ever wrote, more even than is ever explained by what the Religion Clause of the First Amendment actually says. Indeed, anti-Catholicism as such is a huge causal factor. Several scholars, including our own Gerard V. Bradley, have made this case in academic writings. And now Harvard University Press has brought out an important new book by Phillip Hamburger, of the University of Chicago Law School, further documenting the case. And soon, Princeton University Press, in a series I have the honor to edit, will bring out a major study by the great James Hitchcock delivering the final blow. (I should also recommend the Briefs filed by the Becket Fund and by the Catholic League in *Mitchell v. Helms* and *Zelman v. Simmons-Harris,* the recent voucher cases, which contain valuable summaries of the evidence presented at greater detail by Bradley, Hamburger, and Hitchcock.

III.

The question – *Faith under Democracy* – is especially challenging for another reason: any answer is subject to the objection that it proposes a specious or question-begging correlation. Who is to say with confidence that change in this faith, or that has to do with democracy, and not with economic upward mobility, migration, or some other variable factor? I surprise myself by envying those who can do – and even more remarkably to me have the taste to do – regression analysis.

And those are some of the challenges to *description. Evaluation* – for good or ill – introduces additional perils, mostly of the moral, philosophical, and theological kind. Regression analysis won't help there. But at least we are now talking about disciplines I can stake some claim to.

Sometimes we see the problem treated as an evaluation of how faith has fared *throughout the American experience*. But the bigger question is about faith under *democracy*. The questions are not the same. We might have a lively debate about whether America really *is* a democracy. Based upon my contribution to a famous *First Things* symposium a few years back, some say that I think we live, not in any democracy, but under a judicial oligarchy. And, while that is an oversimplification, I do believe that judicial usurpation has damaged American democracy. But I leave that discussion to another occasion.

We might also have a lively debate about when, and to what extent, Americans have talked about America as a *democracy*. Manifestly, our Founders preferred other terms to describe their handiwork, "republic" and "republican" chief among them. I leave aside that discussion, too.

IV.

What I want to address here is this question: when and why did the Supreme Court begin to treat "democracy" (and cognates, including "democratic theory") as *the* political theory of the Constitution, with implications for the religious character of the citizens. Put differently, what did the Court say and do when it decided that there was such as a judicially cognizable thing as a "relationship between faith and democracy". When and why did "democracy" take over the constitutional law of religion? What did it do after it took over?

Here are the answers: (1) it took over during World War II; and (2) "democracy" – as the concept was wielded in the hands of the judges – imposed a secular public sphere; it privatized religion.

Let me explain.

We know that the war against fascism, framed by a wider worry about atheistic communism, called forth among Americans a profound re-commitment to "democracy" (and "freedom"). That was what we were fighting for. We were not fighting for an impersonal system, or for a set of political practices. We fought for "the democratic way of life," a political *culture* with deep roots in character, belief, and psyche. Competent secondary literature – here I draw your attention particularly to the book *After Liberalism*, Paul Gottfried's fine contribution to my Princeton University Press series – explains how "democracy" or ("democratic theory") was splintered into two camps. One group held beliefs much like those articulated in our time by Pope John Paul II: democracy is defensible in moral terms and depends for its legitimacy on the moral values it advances and protects.

The opposing camp saw moral truth as a phantom, a superstition which, when it gained control of citizens' minds, led straight to authoritarianism, if not to outright fascism. These folks favored a pragmatic scientific spirit, and a polite relativism in morals. In the courts and the elite sector of the culture, these folks won. We see, right there in the Supreme Court decisions during and shortly after the war, an explicit link between our "democratic way of life" and secularism, particularly, and in a very aggressive form, in public education.

Here is a nice illustration of the point. It is from the oral argument in *McCollum*, which took place on December 8, 1947, just ten months after the Court in *Everson* declared a constitutional prohibition of any and all government aid to religion, even if the aid was non-discriminatory and non-coercive.

Justice Felix Frankfurter went jaw-to-jaw with the lawyer for the Champaign, Illinois, school district, John Franklin. Franklin's performance at oral argument was audacious, and masterful. He forcefully argued (and proved in his 100-plus page brief) that public authority was free, under the Constitution, to promote religion, so long as there was no discrimination in favor of, or against, particular faiths. This, Franklin said, was what everyone understood *non-establishment* to mean, until the day before yesterday.

An aside: Justice Black, author of the *Everson* stricture, was (the transcript reveals) dumbfounded, tongue-tied, by Franklin's assault upon the *Everson* rule which, it should be said, Franklin correctly described as a *dictum*. It is a wonder *why* – since Black's own penultimate draft for the *Everson* court had taken precisely the same position: to wit, non-establishment meant non-discrimination. In any event, Black produced for the Court no refutation or rejoinder, no rebuttal or counterargument. In full, the Court's response reads: "We are unable to accept th[e] argument. As we stated in *Everson,* we must keep the wall high and impregnable." The *McCollum* Court's imperviousness, or indifference, to evidence and cogent argument is, unfortunately, characteristic of the church-state cases.

Back to the Frankfurter story. Frankfurter made this point to John Franklin, as follows:

> I put my question again: we have a school system of the United States on the one hand, and the relation it has to the democratic way of life. *On the other hand, we have the religious beliefs of our people.* The question is whether any kind of scheme which introduced religious teaching into the public school system is the kind of thing we should have in our democratic institutions (emphasis added).

Frankfurter answered his own question: because *a few* religious groups opposed Champaign's shared time program; for them it was "offensive" and caused "controversy." Its incompatibility with "our democracy" needed no further proof.

The worry at the heart of *McCollum* was most succinctly expressed by Justice Brennan, in the Bible-reading case, *Abington School District v. Schempp,* wherein he referred to the choice "between a public secular education with its uniquely democratic values and some form of private or sectarian education, which offers values of its own." You need look no further for an understanding of Establishment Clause jurisprudence since 1947 – at least the vast swath of it involving K–12 education.

With computer assisted research into Supreme Court opinions since the Founding, one can see at a glance that in the mid-1940's the Court confronted – or constructed – an unprecedented problem concerning religion and democracy. What does that glance reveal? Told to locate all uses of the terms "orthodox" "dogma" "secularism" "irreligion, "no religion," "atheism," "inculcate," and "indoctrinate" the computer search revealed a chasm at around 1943: before then, *almost* none; then the debut of some of these terms followed by dozens of uses, in quick succession. Atheism, for example, appears for the first time in *McCollum*. It has appeared more than 40 times since. The 1940 *Gobitis* case marks the debut of "indoctrinate" and "indoctrination," words which since then have become synonymous with religious teaching. "Orthodoxy"'s career begins with the Second Jehovah's Witness case, *West Virginia v. Barnette*, in 1943. There the Court said: "If there is any fixed star in our constitutional constellation, it is that no official, high or petty, can prescribe what shall be orthodox in politics, nationalism, religion, or other matters of opinion, or force citizens to confess by word or act their faith therein." (but not, interestingly enough, in science, or law!). *Barnette* cited *no* case – none, zero, nil – to support this principle.

By 1944, the Court spoke of our "democratic faith" (in the *Baumgartner* case). In *Prince v. Massachusetts* (the Jehovah's Witness child labor "street preaching" case), the Court stated that "a democratic society rests, for its continuance, upon the growth of a healthy, well-rounded group of young people into full maturity as citizens, with all that implies."

VI.

Because I aim to conclude with a note of challenge to the Court-imposed secularist orthodoxy, I wish to note that it is still very much the governing judicial ideology. Note well: despite some very positive developments since 1990 in the constitutional law of church and state, we still live in *Everson's* world. Under *Lemon v. Kurtzman's* test of constitutionality – battered but still standing – *all* acts of public authority must have a secular purpose and a primary effect which does not advance or aid religion. Aiming to care for and favor religion – even without a trace of favoritism or hostility to any particular religion – is a prohibited "non-secular" purpose. It is unconstitutional per se. In recent years, starting with *Agostini* (in 1997) and on through *Mitchell v. Helms (2000),* the second prong of the *Lemon* test has been made appreciably more sensible. But, according to what remains, the Supreme Court's master principle of church-state law, public authority may do nothing which aids religion as such, or that favors religion over "non-religion" or "irreligion".

Indeed: even as refashioned by *Agostini* and *Helms,* the "effects" test still requires that religious beneficiaries receive favor under a different description, as a member of a class of recipients defined without reference to religion. The advances of recent years, up to and including the vouchers case, have not dislodged this master principle. What we have seen instead is the nearly complete eradication of discrimination against religious speech, institutions, and individuals. In other words, something near a true equality of religion with other forms of belief and expression. The religious speech cases (e.g., *Rosenberger, Good News*) established that free speech of believers is as broad as that of non-believers. The aid cases have been presented as applications of "neutrality" and "private choice" principles.

CONCLUSION

What the civic order – democracy, if that is what you care to call it – hath taken away, might the civic order giveth back?

You have heard a capsule argument for the proposition that the secularist project is a judicially adopted orphan. It has no genuine constitutional pedigree; indeed, no *judicial* lineage to speak of prior to its birth in the crucible of the 1940s. The judicially (or, more comprehensively, the elitist) felt needs of "democracy" gave us secularism as a kind of established religion. Many of us in this room, myself among them, believe that true democracy – and fidelity to the Constitution – instead calls for a basis in faith in the Creator as the ultimate source of fundamental rights and governmental obligations, in objective norms of justice and right, if it is not to degenerate into the domination of the weak by the strong.

Indeed, the problem for the free exercise of religion for Catholics and many other people of faith in the United States today has not been too much democracy, but, rather, too *little*. It has been above all the short-circuiting of democratic deliberation – the judicial imposition in the name of "democracy" of a secularist orthodoxy – that has constrained the ability of Catholics and others to transmit their faith to their children and act on their convictions to shape a public environment – a moral ecology – in line with virtue as they conceive it – and *as they would be prepared to defend it* to their fellow citizens in open deliberation and fair democratic political contestation.

Robert P. George is the McCormick Professor of Jurisprudence, Professor of Politics, and Director of the James Madison Program in American Ideals at Princeton University. Among his interests are theories of law, natural law theories, constitutional law and theory, and problems of religion and politics. His most recent book is *The Clash of Orthodoxies.* He is also the author of *Making Men Moral: Civil Liberties and Public Morality* and *In Defense of Natural Law.* He is the editor of *Natural Law Theory; Natural Law, Liberalism, and Morality;* and *The Autonomy of Law: Essays on Legal Positivism.* He has also published articles in the area of jurisprudence and constitutional law.

He is a member of the editorial board of the *American Journal of Jurisprudence* and of the board of directors of the Philosophy Education Society (which publishes *The Review of Metaphysics*). He has been the recipient of research fellowships from the Howard Foundation and from the Supreme Court of the United States. He served by presidential appointment as a Commissioner on the U.S. Commission for Civil Rights. He holds a law degree from Harvard University and a doctorate in philosopy from Oxford University.

AWARDS BANQUET
THE CARDINAL O'BOYLE AWARD
United States Senator Rick Santorum

The Cardinal O'Boyle Award for 2002 was awarded to U.S. Senator from Pennsylvania Rick Santorum. The presentation was made by incoming Fellowship of Catholic Scholars President, Dean Bernard Dobranski of the Ave Maria Law School, in the following words composed by the Fellowship's Past President, Rev. Ronald Lawler, O.F.M. cap.:

The Fellowship of Catholic Scholars is honored by the presence of Senator Rick Santorum, and is happy to confer on him this award.

As a senator he has been intensely aware of many of the battles that must be fought in public life to guard the dignity and security of our citizens. In a special way, he has been a warrior in defense of the life of the most imperiled of our people, children before their birth.

Senator Santorum was born in Winchester, Virginia, in 1958, but his childhood was spent in Butler, Pennsylvania. He received his undergraduate degree in political science from Pennsylvania State University (whose football team is having a grand resurgence this year!), and he obtained an M.B.A. degree and later a J.D. (law) degree from the University of Pittsburgh.

He first worked in a Pittsburgh law firm, and then was elected to the United States House of Representatives in 1990, at the age of 32. He was first elected a United States Senator in 1994, and was re-elected comfortably in 2000. He has been a hard-working senator, and is a member of some of the most important Senate committees. He is the youngest member of the Senate Republican Leadership. When Congress is in session, he keeps busy with Senate and Senate committee work. During out-of-session times, he goes all over the state – seeing to it that he takes part each year in at least one event in each of Pennsylvania's 65 counties. This may remind us of the days when priests visited the homes of their parishioners with great regularity, keeping an eye on the state of the flock.

He married a member of one of the great Catholic families in western Pennsylvania, Karen Garver. Her father, Dr. Kenneth Garver, at the request of Cardinal Wright, had made a career change in mid-stream, becoming a very distinguished geneticist, and a voice for the Catholic vision of medical ethics in the midst of troubled years. With Karen, Senator Santorum has seven lovely children.

In a special way, I think, the Fellowship is pleased to honor the earnest work that Senator Santorum has faithfully shown in pro-life work. He has shown a Catholic concern also for maintaining a healthy welfare system for the poor; he has been a leader in efforts to serve impoverished rural and urban communities. As a member of the Congressional Empowerment Alliance he has sought to promote responsible fatherhood and marriage. He has been an earnest voice for the public concerns most likely to move us members of the Fellowship.

With his wife Karen, he has not only battled for the lives of unborn children, but with her he showed exemplary courage when faithfulness to principle brings great danger into one's own home. The earnest faith of their home made them able to respond with grace to distressing problems made bitterly personal.

His wife Karen records these struggles in her beautiful little book, *Letters To Gabriel*. At the very time when Senator Santorum was fighting in the Senate against the horror of partial-birth abortions, they learned that their own unborn child, Gabriel, was in great danger, as Karen was also with him. Advice was given to them by their physician to consider an abortion – after all, the mother of other young children had to be saved!

Karen's little book of letters to this son, Gabriel, shows that in the face of personal pressures they did not for a moment consider turning away from their deepest convictions that no one should for any reason deliberately kill another human person. Little Gabriel was born and lived only two hours, all in the arms of his parents, and in each moment received great love. He was baptized; and he died and entered into the great life and love of God.

Senator Santorum is a man of deep and right convictions, a political leader with concern for the most pressing issues of our day. Like Cardinal O'Boyle, after whom this award is named, he knows how to face without flinching the duty to guard principle, even if one must suffer for it. We are happy to present to Senator Rick Santorum the Cardinal O'Boyle Award of the Fellowship of Catholic Scholars.

BEING FAITHFUL, WORKING FAITHFULLY

Remarks by United States Senator Rick Santorum

First and foremost, thank you for this honor.

I am so grateful to be recognized with this particular award because, as a Catholic Senator, I am often faced with questions about my spiritual identity. Your organization is necessary in our society today because you help to define what "Catholic" is. You are engaged on the front lines of the struggle to establish this definition. But the struggle is not centered solely among the intellectuals of the nation's universities; it involves what "Catholic" is in our churches throughout the country, what "Catholic" is in our primary and secondary schools, and certainly what "Catholic" is in our public life. When Americans look at the nation's leading Catholic public figures, they see a range of Catholic models, from Senators Ted Kennedy and Pat Leahy and, yes, Tom Daschle, to Tom Harkin and Barbara Mikulski. Each of these people, in their own way, proclaims that they are Catholic but brings a different meaning to that word. So it becomes so important that you fight to redefine, in America's eyes, what "Catholic" really is – because those of us who seek to be faithful need solid ground on which to stand.

I like to think that I fight the important fights and, again, I thank you for recognizing my work. I cannot think of a role more important to this country or to the world than the mission of this organization. We are the greatest nation the earth has ever known and as such, we have an incredible impact on other countries and cultures. And so, your struggle to set forth what is "Catholic," what is moral, and what is faithful is significant not only to this country, but as a powerful signal to the world. I hope to encourage you and you have my support in your quest.

I would like to share a story with you about how my Catholic faith has motivated me as a United States Senator. We all have stories about the moment we were inspired to stand up for our faith. We were not born with that kind of conviction; we were nurtured along by something or shaken suddenly to stand up and recognize that God was calling us. I am very blessed to have been shaken at the right time and in the right place. It was back in 1996 during the partial-birth abortion debate then taking place in Congress. At that time, I was in my second year as a United States Senator after four years in the House, and I had never said the word "abortion" in a floor debate in either chamber. I had never spoken on the issue. Instead, I had been counseled by all of my advisors that, as a Congressman from a very moderate state, I needed to be careful about these things. I could cast pro-life votes, because it was my conscience to do so, but other than that, I was supposed to be quiet about my position. I was told that I would only serve as a lightning rod if I stood up to fight for the things I internally believed.

I heeded that advice for a long time. And then, one evening, I happened to be in my office listening to the business of the Senate floor on the television. There was a discussion in progress on a subject I had never heard of before called partial-birth abortion. I sat there learning what the procedure was and it became very upsetting to me. I got into a rage that we as a society had gone so far, too far, and I broke. I got pushed to the point where I felt that I needed to say something. I went down to the Senate floor that night and, in a sense, the rest is history. I became engaged in the debate over partial-birth abortion and ultimately I sponsored the bill to ban the procedure, fighting vetoes all the time.

Our son, Gabriel, died during that period of debate over partial-birth abortion. Gabriel, like so many things in my life, clearly showed me that my part in the fight to end partial-birth abortion was God's calling. Gabriel was a great blessing of understanding that helped me to see the beauty and sanctity of life. The experience was horrible, and was something I would never want any other parent to go through. But God blessed us so much with Gabriel's short life. Through Karen's book, and through all that has been written about him, he has blessed so many, touched so many, and saved so many people too.

The second time that the partial-birth abortion bill was considered by the Senate, we knew we were going to lose again, and that we would be unable to override the President's veto. One evening, I was down on the Senate floor, talking about the bill on the last night before the vote was to take place. Time was up on the debate, the Senate was ready to close down for the night, and as I watched the staffers and senators wrap things up, I suddenly felt that I had not finished saying all I needed to say on the subject. I went back into the cloakroom and called Karen at home where she was taking care of our four children, pregnant with our fifth. In the background, through the phone, I could hear the children yelling. It was already eight o'clock in the evening and we live forty minutes away from the

Capitol, and though I should have been on my way home, I told Karen that I was not yet done fighting for the bill, that I still had more to say. Despite the screaming and crying and everything else going on at home, she said: "Well, if that's what you need to do, then that's what you must do."

With that encouragement, I went back to the Senate floor and approached the senator who was sitting in the chair as President pro tempore. The person in the chair at the end of the day is stuck there until everyone is finished speaking. That evening, it happened to be Senator Mike DeWine from Ohio, and I asked him for a few more minutes to talk. I promised him that I really would not be very long, but that I just had to say a little bit more. And then I talked for about an hour and forty-five minutes. I poured my heart out. I talked about my son, I gave examples of other people's experiences, and when I was done, there was nobody left in the chamber. No one was in the gallery. There was nobody, no one besides me and Mike and the man who records all the activity on the Senate floor. At that moment, I never felt more alone. I had just wasted almost two hours of my time, and had left my wife at home with our four screaming kids. I could only think of how wrong of me it was to do that. The next morning we voted, and, as expected, we failed to pass the ban on partial-birth abortion. Despite everything I had done, I did not change a vote.

But I received an incredible blessing. The following Tuesday rolled around and an e-mail from a young man at Michigan State University was sitting on my desk. The young man wrote to explain that he and his girlfriend had been sitting in his apartment on the previous Thursday, flicking through the television channels, when they came across my floor speech on CSPAN2. For some reason, they stopped their channel surfing to listen. They were drawn into what I had to say, the experiences I had to share, and the experiences of others with this abortion procedure.

The young man then wrote: "After a while, I looked over at my girlfriend and she had tears running from her eyes. I asked her what was wrong, and she looked up at me and said: "I'm pregnant and I'm scheduled to have an abortion tomorrow and I wasn't going to tell you."

Today a little girl is now three-and-a-half years old!

What I mean to say to you by telling this story is this: if you are faithful, He will be faithful. On that lonely night, the Holy Spirit moved me to stand up on the Senate floor when it seemed that no one was there to listen because someone I did not see was, in fact, going to hear. It may sometimes be a lonely fight, and it may seem that nobody is listening, but in doing what you do, you are being faithful. That is what matters. Catholics need you in this country, and I need you in my battles. I have the Holy Spirit behind me, and I thank Him tonight for His blessing because it is His great gift that allows me to say and do what I do.

But Catholics, in both public and private life, need you, too. The Holy Spirit has given you these same gifts to speak and to act. So, I ask you, I beg you, listen to Him. God bless you.

THE CARDINAL WRIGHT AWARD
Rev. J. Augustine DiNoia, O.P.

The Cardinal Wright Award for 2002 was awarded in absentia to Father J. Augustine DiNoia, O.P., a member of the International Theological Commission, who has also served as editor-in-chief of *The Thomist* and as Director of the Intercultural Forum at the new John Paul II Cultural Center. Since he had recently been named Undersecretary for the Congregation for the Doctrine of the Faith in Rome, he was unable to be present at the Fellowship convention to receive the award, but sent the following Acceptance to be read:

Twenty-five years ago, a group of Catholic scholars in philosophy, theology, the humanities, and other fields joined together to form the Fellowship of Catholic Scholars. Looking back over the past twenty-five years, the members of the founding group may well be amazed by the great success the Fellowship has enjoyed and the significant contribution it has made to Catholic intellectual life in the United States. Happy to share the joy of the founders and members, the rest of us cannot fail to see as well the hand of divine Providence at work in the foundation and activities of the Fellowship of Catholic Scholars. Almost exactly contemporary with the pontificate of Pope John Paul II, the Fellowship has embraced his teaching and fostered its reception in the United States.

During those years, Pope John Paul II articulated a far-reaching challenge to all Catholic intellectuals and the institutions that sustain them, most notably in *Ex Corde Ecclesiae, Veritatis Splendor,* and

Fides et Ratio. The members of the Fellowship have taken up this challenge, through their teaching, research, and publications, and in this way they have embodied the kinds of collaborators upon which the See of Peter depends for spreading the culture-transforming Gospel of truth and freedom which is Christ's gift to the Church. So it is a great privilege for me to share in this happy moment by being honored with the John Cardinal Wright Award in this twenty-fifth anniversary year of the Fellowship of Catholic Scholars. *Ad multos annos*!

THE FOUNDERS AWARD
Rev. Joseph Fessio, S.J.

The Founders Award for 2002 was awarded to Father Joseph Fessio, S.J.. Now the newly named Chancellor of the new Ave Maria University in Florida, Father Fessio is also the Founder and Editor of Ignatius Press, Director of Religious Books on Tape, Co-founder of both *Adoremus*, the Society for the Renewal of the Sacred Liturgy, and of the Catholic Radio Network. He is the publisher of *The Catholic World Report, Catholic Dossier*, and *Catholic Faith*, among outstanding current Catholic journals. He has taught philosophy at Gonzaga University, the University of Santa Clara, and the University of San Francisco, where he founded the St. Ignatius Institute. He entered the Jesuit novitiate in September, 1961, and was ordained to the priesthood in June, 1972. He holds a B.A. and M.A. in philosophy from Gonzaga University, a Master's in theology from Lyons, France, and a Doctorate in theology from the University of Regensburg in Germany, where he studied under Cardinal Joseph Ratzinger.

PRESIDENTIAL FORUM
25th Anniversary
Fellowship of Catholic Scholars Convention

Presidential Remarks
Rev. Thomas F. Dailey, O.S.F.S., S.T.D.

It is my pleasure to welcome you to this panel presentation, which we have arranged as a special event for our 25th annual FCS convention. In preparing for this convention, we certainly wanted to celebrate our anniversary, and so we tried to create ways in which to honor the work of our Fellowship.

We considered having a "roast" of certain notable members . . . but we only have one weekend to work with! So, instead, we devised this panel of some of our past presidents as a way of celebrating the living memory of our founders. After all, one notable feat of our Fellowship is that no FCS president has ever passed away! More importantly, these are the men on whose shoulders the Fellowship has been carried for these past 25 years. Their memory is ours. And we thought it would be good to hear from them. In fact, I've asked each of them to share his thoughts on two questions: What is the Fellowship's greatest accomplishment in our first 25 years? And what is the biggest challenge that our Fellowship faces as we begin the next 25 years?

From my perspective, the Fellowship is noteworthy precisely because of the work of these legends on our stage. And not only do we have these past presidents, but there are also several of our Cardinal Wright Award winners with us this weekend. These persons have provided invaluable service to the Church in their promotion of Catholic teaching. They are giants in our midst. We are proud to share Fellowship with them and to collaborate in their work of providing Catholic scholarship to our culture.

It is precisely there, in the notion of "culture," that the work of the Fellowship has made its mark. It is there that the work of the Fellowship remains most in need. In our present culture, faith suffers from two delusions. On the one hand, people regard faith as a "private" matter, one relegated to the realm of subjective and personal choice. In such an individualistic view, faith has little or no social impact; in fact, many believe that faith plays no part in the public square.

On the other hand, people look upon faith with "indifferent" eyes, believing, as it were, that generic faith in a God is all that matters, regardless of the conception of that God or the content of that belief. In such a pluralistic view, faith has little or no claim to adherence or to truth; in fact, many believe that one religion is as good as any other and we believers should all just learn to get along.

Needless to say, the Fellowship of Catholic Scholars does not share these cultural delusions. Our Catholic faith is corporate in nature, issuing from and contributing to the Body of Christ that we know is the Church. Our Catholic faith makes truth claims that have profound existential and social consequences. Our work as scholars is to elucidate these truths and their consequences in such a way as to promote the common good of humanity.

Illustrative of the need for this scholarly work in the faith is the current "crisis" that the church in the USA is undergoing. In my judgment, this crisis is not, fundamentally, a matter of aberrant behavior endemic to the priesthood. Though it is no reason to dismiss the gravity of the situation, the actual percentage of clerics engaging in sexual abuse of minors is relatively small, no different than that of the general population, in fact. The behavior of such a minority is not the real problem. Nor is the crisis about leadership in the Church. Clearly the actions of some bishops in the handling of the abusers and their victims have been lamentable. And it is true that bishops should be less concerned about public relations and/or financial security and more concerned about shepherding their flocks. Still, these remain "administrative" matters.

The real crisis, as I see it, is one of teaching. Where the failure has occurred is in the public arena of courageously proclaiming the truths of the faith and steadfastly accepting those truths as determinative for human living. That "evangelical" failure leads, necessarily, to crisis – a crisis of belief, in which the Church now suffers from a lack of credibility, and a crisis of behavior, by which members of the Church have become public sinners.

But this very crisis points to the ongoing need for the work of our Fellowship of Catholic Scholars. Beyond recalling the failures of the past and lamenting the situations which have lead to the present crisis, our Fellowship can and must look forward to the "new springtime" which our Holy Father reminds us has already begun in the saving action of Christ's incarnation and redemption. How this turning point in human history can and should impact our contemporary culture is the focal point of our mission as a Fellowship of Catholic Scholars. To bring this "new springtime" into fuller blossom, we need, in my view, to re-focus our efforts on each of the pillars of our organization.

First, we need a renewed attention to the promotion of our *Fellowship itself.* For 25 years, this organization has provided necessary and beneficial support to those scholars laboring by faith, particularly when their adherence to the faith has come under fire. Now, as a new generation of Catholic scholars appears on the intellectual and cultural scenes, we need to devise ways in which to recruit new members to our organization. This is every fellowship member's task if we are to remain in existence.

Second, we need a renewed awareness of our *Catholic* communion. For 25 years, the Fellowship has been a stalwart champion of fidelity to the teachings of the Church, as we should be, even when that fidelity creates suffering and necessitates sacrifice. Indeed, this fidelity has been and remains the distinctive dimension to our work. Yet, as we seek to defend the faith, we must remain cognizant of the fact that we do not define the faith. As we champion orthodox thought and moral living, we must also practice virtue ourselves, including humility and gentleness. Ours has been and will be the task of being critical with regard to distortions of the truth. But doing the truth in love, as our faith requires of us, challenges us to be critical without ridicule. The language that we use, not only of others' thought but, by implication, of others' character, should be charitable, lest we cast aside those very persons, us included, whom faith is meant to save. We should adopt as a principle the dictum of St.

Francis de Sales (Bishop and Doctor of the Church), who, in his work as one of the Church's foremost apologists, reminds us that "a truth spoken without charity comes from a charity that is not true."

Finally, we need a renewed effort at disseminating our work as *Scholars*. For 25 years, the Fellowship has produced valuable scholarship in terms of the presentations and publications of our members. The work of many individuals has left a treasury of Catholic thought to the lasting benefit of our Church and our society. Yet, as we move into the new millennium, we need to take greater advantage of the mechanisms by which orthodox Catholic thought can be shared with others. Our *FCS Quarterly* reaches an important audience, including all of our bishops and presidents of all our Catholic colleges and universities. But it still must grow, especially in terms of the number and quality of articles being published. Our website offers numerous resources in a format that makes them available virtually worldwide. But it must be more appealing, in terms of accessible content and increased usage. Our annual conventions offer a public venue for scholarly engagement with significant issues affecting our faith and culture. But these too must be more prominent, in terms of dealing with important and even controversial topics, and also in terms of reaching a broader audience of members and non-members alike.

Rightly does our Fellowship of Catholic Scholars celebrate 25 years of service to the Church. Looking backward, the legends in our midst should be remembered for their invaluable contributions. And, looking forward, we should renew and reaffirm our commitment to providing solid Catholic scholarship in the promotion of our faith. In this way, we will participate in and contribute to that "springtime" of the Christian life, of the human spirit, and of hope that the Church invites each of us and all our culture to behold.

Gerard V. Bradley

Father Dailey asked each of us to identify the Fellowship's greatest accomplishment to date, and to pick out a very significant challenge in the days ahead. It is a look behind and ahead, at a particularly painful and maybe pivotal moment in the life of the American Church. The most *startling* accomplishment of the Fellowship is easy to identify: no one who ever served as President of the Fellowship has ever died! I do not mean that no President has died in office, the way FDR did. I mean that every single President is still rattling around in the Church Militant. This, despite the fact that several worthies ascended to presidential heights already in their sunset years, members of AARP and eligible for free coffee at McDonald's. For myself, I freely confess that I have cancelled my life insurance.

It is difficult, I also confess, more seriously, to pick out one achievement or event in the life of the Fellowship as the *greatest* of accomplishments. I do not know much about the Fellowship's early years. A wise-guy student myself in those years, most of what I know has been learned at the footstools of the greats who were Present at the Creation, including a couple of the men seated beside me now. If I look only to my own six-year turn at the helm, our work in favor of implementing *Ex Corde Ecclesiae* has to have been our most valuable undertaking. The Fellowship contributed in diverse ways: individual members talked and wrote and organized on their home campuses; many of us published scholarly or journalistic articles on the matter; and as a corporate body the Fellowship intervened in the bishops' deliberations on Canon 812 (the *mandatum*) and on other contested matters.

The story has had a bittersweet ending. Despite our efforts, ECE is currently almost dead in the water, undermined or neglected by many bishops and colleges, even before episcopal attention got diverted to less edifying crises. But in the history that shall be written of Catholic colleges' descent into secularity, there will certainly be a few paragraphs on the Fellowship – prescient, faithful, and standing at the post!

The most significant challenge before us is the same: to stay the course, to remain steadfast, to hold tight the reins. I think it will be harder to do that over the coming years. Notwithstanding the title of these proceedings, I myself do not see the coming years as a *springtime* for the Church, at least not in these United States. Episcopal leadership is crippled for perhaps a generation. During that time America's bishops (as a whole: of course there will be notable exceptions, perhaps more than a few) will cleave tenaciously to some imagined non-ideological Catholic middle. Given the way these things work, the Fellowship and others of its persuasion will be assigned its usual place on the "right" (and I do not mean by that "correct"). We will continue to be on the outside, looking in, as well as marginalized, partisan. Our interventions will rarely be welcomed by the bishops.

Of course this is only the view looking at the Chancery. There are other views. The challenge of the coming years may be to re-dedicate the Fellowship to its founding principles, and to implement them as independently as possible. Assume little or no support from the hierarchy. Assume continued hostility from the mainstream Catholic colleges, publishing houses, professional associations, and such. Assume that secular observers will have an auto key which adds to every mention of the FCS words such as "extreme," "right-wing," "ultramontane," "conservative," and the like. Assume further, though, that all this does not matter, and then simply go on to the apostolate that *does* matter!

Rev. Kenneth Baker, s.j.

When I first heard of the formation of the Fellowship of Catholic Scholars, I was immediately interested. Consequently, I went to the first organizing meeting out in the cornfields near Kansas City. At the meeting, I was surprised to see some people there that I did not expect to see.

An important part of the history of the Fellowship has been giving us all the chance to know each other better. This has been our version of "networking."

The annual meetings have been intellectually challenging and emotionally encouraging. They remind me of a letter I once received, directed to me as editor of *The Homiletic &Pastoral Review*. The priest told me that he felt isolated in his state and sometimes thought he was crazy because he disagreed with much that was going on in the diocese. Then, every month he received his HPR, and he discovered that there were many priests around the country who agreed with him in support of the magisterium of the Church. The Fellowship has been something like that.

Over the years our members have produced some fine scholarly work. I have frequently published articles by members of the Fellowship, including Msgr. George A. Kelly, Msgr. William B. Smith, James Hitchcock, Janet Smith, Fr. Leonard Kennedy, c.s.b., Donald DeMarco, and others.

Over the years, the U.S. Conference of Catholic Bishops has tended to ignore us, but several bishops have privately sought help and advice from some of our members. The USCCB itself has not sought our help, but they know we are here!

The Fellowship generates hope for all of us because we are seeking the truth of the Catholic faith under the guidance of the magisterium. I am proud to be a member – and past president – of this Fellowship, and to have been able to associate with you over the past 25 years. Let us hope and pray that the next 25 years will be even more fruitful than the past 25 years!

Msgr. George A. Kelly

The most shocking question ever asked of me – or at least one of them! – was posed to me in 1973 by French Cardinal Gabriel Garrone, who was then Prefect for Catholic Education under Pope Paul VI. Cardinal Garrone asked me, "Is there no other voice for Catholic higher education in the United States than that of the Jesuits or of Notre Dame?"

At that point Cardinal Garrone had just completed five years of failure to restore Catholic colleges and universities to their birthright. At a world Congress of presidents of Catholic colleges and universities held in Rome in 1972, the French cardinal had encountered open rebellion from the Church on the part of, among others, the presidents of Georgetown and Notre Dame in the United States, who told the Roman authorities to their faces that American college presidents would no longer accept – either from the pope or the bishops – any Church norms for the running of their schools. Going back to the 1967 Land O' Lakes statement issued by 26 such Catholic college and university presidents in the small Wisconsin town of that name – a statement that called for complete "institutional autonomy and academic freedom" for Catholic higher education institutions – these educators understood their defiance of Rome to mean that their institutions also eschewed the task of institutionally transmitting or maintaining the Catholic faith and its way of life.

Instead, Catholic colleges and universities in the United States had decided to adopt the "secular" model of the typical American university as their own, while keeping the name "Catholic." Orthodox faith and morals would henceforth be matters of free choice for administrators, faculty, and students. It was a strange turn for the Catholic Church in the United States, to be sure. The first president of Georgetown had proudly announced in 1798: "The directors of this institution openly profess that they have nothing so much at heart as to implant virtue, and destroy in their pupils the seeds of vice." "Success in this alone," he added, would be "an ample award for their incessant endeavors."

In 1960, the best practicing Catholics, like many priests and nuns, were Catholic college graduates. By 1972 this was no longer true. Cardinal Garrone, as if in desperation at the spectacle of 230-odd Catholic colleges and universities in the United States no longer committed institutionally to passing on the truths revealed by Jesus Christ, turned to us, and asked: "Can you really help us out?" It was then that the seeds of the Fellowship of Catholic Scholars were planted. The Fellowship was an idea whose time had come.

The French cardinal was as mad as two wet hens at the gall of the "Land O' Lakers." When they returned to America from the 1972 Congress, they actually made a public claim that Rome agreed with them about their declaration of independence and autonomy from the hierarchy. Cardinal Garrone understood very well, however, that it was a veritable chasm that separated the rebellion he was faced with from "the obedience of faith" (Rom 1:5). He also knew the harm that would result to the faith of the young, and to aspiring priests and religious.

The Collapse of Church Authority

Is it not strange that in one year, 1967, there were no less than three successful rebellions staged against the authority of the hierarchy? Land O' Lakes was one of them; the other two were the Catholic University student and faculty strike against the school's attempt to get rid of dissenting theologian Father Charles Curran, and the rebellion of the Immaculate Heart of Mary nuns in Los Angeles. In all three of these cases the hierarchy blinked. Philadelphia Archbishop John Krol, then vice-president of the bishops' conference, thought that Father Curran ought to be fired from the Catholic University, yet later only moaned that it was useless to be a bishop or a university board member if one could not terminate for good cause a young, untenured theology professor. Around the same time, Washington Cardinal Patrick O'Boyle, asked about what had happened to bring on such a crisis, replied: "We ate crow!" Cardinal McIntyre in Los Angeles, and the California bishops, equivalently had to tell then bishops' conference president

Archbishop John Dearden of Detroit to mind his own business; it turned out that the latter had written to Rome seeking *leniency* for the rebellious Los Angeles nuns!

Even the bishops called to Rome for the first World Synod of Bishops in 1967 were so alarmed at "the abuses and deviations" in doctrine, liturgy, and pastoral practice they were seeing that they recommended strongly warning "rash and imprudent" offenders against the faith and removing the "pertinacious." Five years later, in 1972, Franjo Cardinal Seper, then prefect of the Congregation for the Doctrine of the Faith, blamed the bishops for the Church's troubles. Rome was too far away to cope with local scandals, he said, especially if "we get no cooperation from the bishops."

It was while we were meeting with Cardinal Garrone that we also happened to meet Bishop Fulton J. Sheen, who wanted to know what we were doing in Rome. We told him. To which he responded: "I tell my relatives with college-age students to send them to secular colleges where they will have to fight for their faith, rather than to Catholic colleges where it will be stolen from them."

Calling of the Guard

The assembling of our Catholic apologist troops around the Fellowship took some time. Some outstanding Jesuits were among the first volunteers: Francis Canavan, Paul Quay, John Ford, Joseph Mangan, Earl Weiss, Cornelius Buckley, Joseph Fessio, Robert Brunge, Donald Keefe, James Schall, Kenneth Baker, Joseph Farrahar, and others. When Cardinal Cooke was told that the Jesuits were going to save the Church, he replied: "You must be kidding!" But some prominent lay scholars came in early too: William May, J. Brian Benestad, John Finnis, Germain Grisez, Glenn Olsen, Drs.Eugene Diamond and William Lynch, James Hitchcock, John Hittinger, John Kippley, Russell Shaw, Brian Harrison, John Guegen, Charles Dechert, and yet others. Then there were the priests such as William Smith, Henry Sattler, James Turro, Robert Levis, and Michael Wrenn. Outstanding too were religious women such as Sisters Hannah Klaus, Assumpta Long, and Joan Gormley. Father Ronald Lawler, O.F.M. Cap., then at Catholic University, was elected our first president.

While the Fellowship was in formation (from 1974 on), the Catholic Theological Society of the United States (CTSA), an episcopal stand-by, had commissioned and was having prepared a book *Human Sexuality*, which subsequently dispensed every thinking (or non-thinking!) Catholic from the absolute demands of the Sixth Commandment. Budding Fellowship members such as Henry Sattler, C.SS.R., and Joseph Farraher, S.J., as CTSA members, tried to side-track *Human Sexuality*, but were denied recognition. This outrageous book, published in 1977, the year of the Fellowship's founding, was condemned by the American bishops; yet its thinking made its way widely through publicity in the secular press and in journals such as *The National Catholic Reporter.* Although *Human Sexuality* demonstrated how badly true Catholic apologists were needed, the episcopal bureaucracy showed little interest in Fellowship help, even after Father Lawler had met with the General Secretary of the bishops' conference. Two years later, then President James Hitchcock encountered the same lack of interest.

From the outset, the Fellowship, through its *Newsletter*, which later became a *Quarterly*, became a strong voice in support of the Church's teaching office. 1977 turned out to be a good year for this, since it was in that year that the American bishops published a *National Catechetical Directory*, which the theological establishment had tried to sabotage, but which the Fellowship helped keep on the right track (ultimately the document had to undergo specific corrections in Rome before it could be issued). After his election the Fellowship issued a call for research scholars to speak out in defense of Pope John Paul II and his teachings.

Also from the outset, the Fellowship came to the aid of Catholic scholars under fire in their own institutions because of their orthodoxy; contested the National Catholic Education Association and its views on Catholic higher education (1979); defended the censure of Father Hans Küng by the Congregation for the Doctrine of the Faith (1980); and challenged the Catholic Biblical Association on its study of priestly ordination (1980). These were only some of the efforts undertaken by the Fellowship and its members in the early days of the organization.

In the 25 years of the existence of the organization, Fellowship members have flooded the market with important Catholic articles and books, both scholarly and for the general reader. It is not possible to do anything but mention a *few* of these books here, with apologies to those Fellowship members whose works do not get mentioned. To begin in alphabetical order with just a few of the volumes immediately available on my own shelves: Kenneth Baker, S.J., *Inside the Bible* (1998); Gerard Bradley, *Church-State Relationships in America* (1987); Francis Canavan, S.J., *Pins in the Liberal Balloon* (1990); Donald DeMarco, *The Heart of Virtue* (1996); John Finnis, *Natural Law and Natural Rights*; Robert George, *Making Men Moral: Civil Liberties and Public Morality* (1993); Germain Grisez, *The Way of the Lord Jesus* (Vol. 1, 1983, with subsequent volumes following); John F. Harvey, O.S.F.S., *The Homosexual Person;* James Hitchcock, *Catholicism and Modernity: Confrontation or Capitulation* (1979); Helen Hull Hitchcock, *The Politics of Prayer: Feminist Language and the Worship of God* (1992); Donald J. Keefe, S.J., *Covenantal Theology: The Eucharistic Order of History* (1991); Msgr. George A. Kelly, *The Battle for the American Church* (1979); Joyce Little, *The Church and the Culture War: Secular Anarchy or Sacred Order* (1995); William May, *Marriage: The Rock on which the Family Is Built* (1995); Ralph McInerny, *What Went Wrong with Vatican II?* (1998); Paul Quay, S.J., *The Christian Meaning of Human Sexuality* (1985); Patrick Riley, *Civilizing Sex: On Chastity and the Common Good* (2000); H. Vernon Sattler, C.Ss.R., *Sex Education in the Catholic Family* (1984); James Schall, S.J., *Does Catholicism Still Exist?* (1994); Russell Shaw, *Papal Primacy in the Third Millennium* (2000); Mary Shivanandan, *Crossing the Threshold of Love: A New Vision of Marriage* (1999); Janet Smith, *Humanae Vitae: A Generation Later* (1991); Joseph Varacalli, *Bright Promise, Failed Community: Catholics and the American Public Order* (2000); Kenneth Whitehead, *One, Holy, Catholic, and Apostolic: The Early Church Was the Catholic Church* (2000); and Michael Wrenn, *Catechisms and Controversies: Religious Education in the Postconciliar Years* (1991).

A Silver Jubilee

The Fellowship of Catholic Scholars, now twenty-five years old, is an important part of a Catholic counter-revolution against the secularism that overtook the Church during the 1960s. Other entities and organizations, more or less "allied" with the Fellowship in the same cause, have worked towards the same end of upholding the integrity of the truths of the faith. Father Joseph Fessio and his Ignatius Press led the way, followed in short order by Helen Hull

Hitchcock and her Women for Faith and Family. John and Sheila Kippley's Couple to Couple League helped keep alive an important traditional Catholic witness to the integrity of marriage. Stephen Krason and Joseph Varacalli performed a great service in organizing the Society of Catholic Social Scientists, as did Patrick Reilly and his collaborators in the Cardinal Newman Society. Also, the founders and teachers in the new, "orthodox" Catholic colleges, now number-ing more than a half dozen, have similarly helped keep alive the authentic Catholic tradition in difficult times while contributing to the "restoration" of Pope John Paul II.

Protestant Christianity, which once underpinned American soci-ety, in the nineteenth century, proved helpless to impede its Harvards, Princetons, and Yales from abandoning their religious and Christian roots in exchange for power, status, and wealth in capital-istic America. The Protestant "crusade" of that day, which thought it could guarantee that papists might not apply for equal social status, learned in short order that an earlier generation of American Catholic bishops were quite effective in building up their faith structures – like the building up of some 230-odd Catholic colleges and univer-sities! By the time World War II came along, it was "Catholic power" that begot anxiety among the secular potentates. Mainline Protestant Christian culture was disappearing, and secularist concern about this brought into existence such anti-Catholic organizations as Protestants and Other Americans United for the Separation of Church and State, and, later, People for the American Way.

Just as Catholicism was beginning to be respectable, however, and practicing Catholics were beginning to appear prominently on corporate boards and in government bureaus, the leaders of the Catholic colleges and universities chose to follow Harvard, Princeton, and Yale and depart from the Georgetown vision of 1789 – that is, they abandoned the idea of maintaining an institutional commitment, not only to academic learning, but to learning God's truth and His way of life as well. Since academics, more than bureau-crats, tend to set the tone for American public opinion, the greatest threat to the Catholic faith system today thus lies in the Church's own complex of higher education.

Rome has been attempting to deal with this problem for over thir-ty years, and, eventually, Pope John Paul II established his *Ex Corde Ecclesiae* as the law for the likes of today's Georgetowns and Notre

Dames. ECE demands institutional commitment to Catholicism, truly believing faculty and administrators, and visible Church discipline. The Fellowship, especially under the leadership of its then President Gerry Bradley (1995–2001), worked hard to support this same vision and the efforts of the committee headed by Anthony Cardinal Bevilacqua of Philadelphia to put in place a valid American Application of *Ex Corde Ecclesiae*. Unfortunately, although this ECE Application is now officially in place, the work itself still awaits its final fulfillment. For the moment, ECE remains a dead letter in America, and Catholic higher education still remains the Church's most dangerous foe.

In 1938, Hilaire Belloc wrote his book *The Great Heresies* in which – without any knowledge of or regard for the emerging powerhouse called American Catholicism – he identified godless secularism as the most dangerous heresy in the Church's long history. Why is the Church today confronting this heresy so much less vigorously than she once confronted Arianism or Protestantism? That is part of our dilemma.

Somebody has to show the way, of course. Fortunately, Pope John Paul II has provided us with the kind of leadership we need. But somebody has to respond to the pope's call, too. That is where we come in! As one academic recently prayed aloud: "Thank God for the Fellowship of Catholic Scholars"!

APPENDIX:
FELLOWSHIP OF CATHOLIC SCHOLARS

Membership Information:
Christopher.Janosik@villanova.edu

Statement of Purpose

We, Catholic Scholars in various disciplines, join in fellowship in order to serve Jesus Christ better, by helping one another in our work and by putting our abilities more fully at the service of the Catholic faith.

We wish to form a Fellowship of Catholic Scholars who see their intellectual work as expressing the service they owe to God. To Him we give thanks for our Catholic faith and for every opportunity He gives us to serve that faith.

We wish to form a Fellowship of Catholic Scholars open to the work of the Holy Spirit within the Church. Thus we wholeheartedly accept and support the renewal of the Church of Christ undertaken by Pope John XXIII, shaped by Vatican Council II, and carried on by succeeding popes.

We accept as the rule of our life and the thought the entire faith of the Catholic Church. This we see not merely in solemn definitions but in the ordinary teaching of the pope and the bishops in union with him, and also embodied in those modes of worship and ways of Christian life, of the present as of the past, which have been in harmony with the teaching of St. Peter's successors in the See of Rome.

- To contribute to this sacred work, our Fellowship will strive to:
- Come to know and welcome all who share our purpose;
- Make known to one another our various competencies and interests;
- Share our abilities with one another unstintingly in our efforts directed to our common purpose;

- Cooperate in clarifying the challenges which must be met;
- Help one another to evaluate critically the variety of responses which are proposed to these challenges;
- Communicate our suggestions and evaluations to members of the Church who might find them helpful;
- Respond to requests to help the Church in her task of guarding the faith as inviolable and defending it with fidelity;
- Help one another to work through, in scholarly and prayerful fashion and without public dissent, any problem which may arise from magisterial teaching.

With the grace of God for which we pray, we hope to assist the whole Church to understand her own identity more clearly, to proclaim the joyous gospel of Jesus more confidently, and to carry out its redemptive to all humankind more effectively.

To apply for membership, contact:

Dr. Christopher Janosik
FCS Executive Secretary
Villanova University
304 St. Augustine Center
Villanova, PA 19085
TEL: 610-519-7295
FAX: 610-519-5643
E-MAIL: Christopher.Janosik@villanova.edu

Member Benefits

Fellowship of Catholic Scholars Quarterly – All members receive four issues annually. This approximately 50-page publication includes:

President's Page
Scholarly articles
Important Documentation
Bulletin Board (news)
Book Reviews
Occasional Fellowship symposia

National Conventions – All members are invited to attend this annual gathering, held in various cities where, by custom, the local ordinary greets and typically celebrates Mass for the members of the Fellowship. The typical convention program includes:

Daily Mass

Keynote Address
At least six scholarly Sessions
Banquet and Awards
Membership business meeting and occasional substantive meetings on subjects of current interest to the Fellowship's membership
Current members receive a copy of the published *Proceedings,*
containing the texts of the speeches of each national convention,
with other material of interest sometimes included.

NATIONAL AWARDS

The Fellowship grants the following awards, usually presented
during the annual convention.

The Cardinal Wright Award – given *annually* to a Catholic
adjudged to have done an outstanding service for the Church in the
tradition of the late Cardinal John J. Wright, Bishop of Pittsburgh
and later Prefect of the Congregation for the Clergy in Rome. The
recipients of this Award have been:

1979 – Rev. Msgr. George A. Kelly
1980 – Dr. William E. May
1981 – Dr. James Hitchcock
1982 – Dr. Germain Grisez
1983 – Rev. John Connery, S.J.
1984 – Rev. John A. Hardon, S.J.
1985 – Dr. Herbert Ratner
1986 – Dr. Joseph P. Scottino
1987 – Rev. Joseph Farraher, S.J., & Rev. Joseph Fessio, S.J.
1988 – Rev. John Harvey, O.S.F.S.
1989 – Dr. John Finnis
1990 – Rev. Ronald Lawler, O.F.M. Cap.
1991 – Rev. Francis Canavan, S.J.
1992 – Rev. Donald J. Keefe, S.J.
1993 – Dr. Janet E. Smith
1994 – Dr. Jude P. Dougherty
1995 – Rev. Msgr. William B. Smith
1996 – Dr. Ralph McInerny
1997 – Rev. James V. Schall, S.J.
1998 – Rev. Msgr. Michael J. Wrenn & Mr. Kenneth D.
Whitehead
1999 – Dr. Robert P. George

2000 – Dr. Mary Ann Glendon
2001 – Thomas W. Hilgers, M.D.
2002 – Rev. J. Augustine DiNoia, O.P.

The Cardinal O'Boyle Award – This award is given occasionally to individuals who actions demonstrate a courage and witness in favor of the Catholic faith similar to that exhibited by the late Cardinal Patrick A. O'Boyle, Archbishop of Washington, in the face of the pressures of our contemporary society which tend to undermine the faith. The recipients of this award have been:

1988 – Rev. John C. Ford, S.J.
1991 – Mother Angelica, P.C.P.A., EWTN
1995 – John and Sheila Kippley, Couple to Couple League
1997 – Rep. Henry J. Hyde (R-IL)
2002 – Senator Rick Santorum (R-PA)

The Founder's Award – Given *occasionally* to individuals with a record of outstanding service in defense of the Catholic faith and in support of the Catholic intellectual life. In 2002 the award was presented to the Rev. Joseph Fessio, S.J.

PRESIDENTS OF THE FELLOWSHIP

2002– Dean Bernard Dobranski, Ave Maria Law School
2001–2002 Rev. Thomas F. Dailey, O.S.F.S., DeSales University
1993–2001 Prof. Gerard V. Bradley, Notre Dame Law School
1991–1995 Prof. Ralph McInerny, University of Notre Dame
1989–1991   Rev. Kenneth Baker, S.J., *Homiletic & Pastoral Review*
1987–1989   Prof. William E. May, John Paul II Institute on Marriage and the Family
1985–1987 Rev. Msgr. George A. Kelly, Archdiocese of New York
1983–1985 Rev. Earl Weiss, S.J., Loyola University
1981–1983 Rev. Msgr. William B. Smith, St. Joseph's Seminary, Yonkers, New York
1979–1981 Prof. James Hitchcock, St. Louis University
1977–1979 Rev. Ronald Lawler, O.F.M. Cap., Diocese of